D0090328

Womanspirit

BOOKS BY THE AUTHOR

A Practical Guide to Spiritual Reading
Approaching the Sacred
Blessings That Make Us Be
Celebrating the Single Life
Meditation in Motion
Pathways of Spiritual Living
Renewed at Each Awakening
Steps Along the Way
The Journey Homeward
Womanspirit

Co-authored with Adrian van Kaam:

Am I Living a Spiritual Life?
Commitment: Key to Christian Maturity
Songs for Every Season
Tell Me Who I Am
The Emergent Self
The Participant Self

WOMANSPIRIT

Reclaiming the Deep Feminine in Our Human Spirituality

Susan Muto

CROSSROAD • NEW YORK

To the great women I have known,
living and dead,
in texts and through times of testing,
as writers, friends, relatives, and colleagues,
I lovingly dedicate this book.

1991

The Crossroad Publishing Company
370 Lexington Avenue, New York, NY 10017

Copyright © 1991 by Susan Muto

Printed in the United States of America
Typesetting output: TEXSource, Houston

Library of Congress Cataloging-in-Publication Data

Muto, Susan Annette.
    Womanspirit : reclaiming the deep feminine in our human
spirituality / Susan Muto.
        p. cm.
    Includes bibliographical references.
    ISBN 0-8245-1129-8
    1. Women, Catholic—Religious life. 2. Women, Christian—
Religious life. I. Title.
BX2353.M87 1991
248'.082—dc20
                                      91-21016
                                          CIP

Contents

Acknowledgments

I WANT TO ACKNOWLEDGE with particular warmth and love the women who responded to the questionnaire I sent out when I first began to work on this book. Their names will remain understandably anonymous to protect their privacy; their narratives and reflections were invaluable to me. What they had to say complemented in a wise, gentle, and challenging way my own offerings. To the women whose spirit remains in me, my grandmother and mother, thanks is too small a word. Male and female friends and relatives have stood by me during these times of self-disclosure and have encouraged me to bring this book — perhaps more than any other I have written — to completion. I must cite in a special way in this regard my co-author of many books, my eminent colleague, Father Adrian van Kaam, C.S.Sp., Ph.D., who is known to me and many as a man truly supportive of "womanspirit." Last but not least, I offer a word of heartfelt gratitude to Marilyn Russell, my excellent secretary and typist of this manuscript, and to Michael Leach, my editor and publisher at Crossroad Publishing Company, who knew from the start that this was one book that had to be written through me. I love and thank you all.

Introduction

WHO ARE WE AS WOMEN? How do we perceive ourselves? Why have so many books been written about us? Why do we need another? My answers to these questions do not resemble the remote speculations of a dispassionate observer, who analyzes behavior from a distance like a specialist investigating the causes of disease without knowing patients who suffer. These questions are in all honesty my own: Who am I? How do I perceive myself? Can I or any woman of faith fathom the answer?

I was seeking clarity in the midst of ambiguity when I began to write what turned out to be a dialogue between my own experiences and the testaments of faith I received from women I interviewed by mail and phone, from women whose writings I came to know through research and reading, and from women who are close friends and family members. Their words, often quoted directly in the chapters to follow, prevented this book from becoming merely an exercise in autobiography and turned it into what is also an objective treatment of women's concerns for self and others, for life and world at home, in the workplace, in the church, and in society.

I have been listening to women's concerns for many years in my role as principal writer for the Drafting Committee of the National Council of Catholic Bishops' proposed pastoral response to women, the first draft of which was entitled "Partners in the Mystery of Redemption" (1988). The more recent draft, designated as "One in Christ Jesus" (1990), is to date still undergoing revision. My involvement with this remarkable process of data collection, periodic meetings, writing and rewriting, listening and responding has given me a privileged opportunity to pay attention in a non-judgmental, open manner to the many voices of women, to reflect on our common concerns, especially in the realm of spirituality, and to attempt now in this book to offer a personal response.

Had I listened to my own misgivings, this book might never have been written. It was inspired by heart-to-heart communications with women friends I had come to know through their classical writings, shining lights of the past like Catherine of Siena, Julian of Norwich, and Teresa of Avila as well as women in the present from whom I received intimate letters, journal accounts, and soul-searching answers to the questionnaire I sent to a select group.

My intention was to follow in detail the formative experiences of Catholic Christian women, not to study our faith tradition as such. This book is not about the theology of the feminine nor about the psychology, sociology, or anthropology of women, yet elements of these disciplines are present, woven into the fabric of experience that binds the book together.

Sociological or theological approaches to women in the church are available from the pens of excellent scholars. The writings of Christian feminists offer new and challenging interpretations of scripture, but I had another aim in mind: to come to know faithful women from the viewpoint of our daily lived spirituality, from our sense of being in the process of formation, reformation, and transformation from birth to death.

If the book at times meanders, it is not by mistake. The text reflects how my mind was working as I listened to women tell me stories with no expectations of foreseen conclusions. Hence the writing is by design open-ended. I am pleased with the results, though this book's ultimate efficacy is for my readers to decide. I do see what has emerged as a contribution to the spirituality of women, ranging from seemingly insignificant glimpses of history to disclosures of intimate personal and religious experiences.

While this is one book, it is made up of many parts arranged like patchwork pieces of cloth that, when sewn together, disclose a distinct pattern. Writing it was like looking through a kaleidoscope. Every time I lifted a new facet of *womanspirit* into the light, the sentences would swirl around and rearrange themselves in fresh narrative and discursive forms. So unique were its emerging designs and disclosures that I found myself discovering what I wanted to say and remember only while actually putting pen to paper.

I felt in truth like an explorer following a treasure map without knowing for sure if its indicators were accurate. I wondered occasionally where I was going and how the bits and pieces of my life and the lives of countless Christian women were connected. Surprisingly, there were common themes and threads amidst the diversity of my own and others' experience. I was being led not only to a destination but to a meeting with my own destiny.

All that I have seen and heard convinces me that women are powerful witnesses to the faith to which our foremothers and fathers held fast. Women who believe do not need proof. We know that Jesus Christ has confirmed the dignity of our personhood and called us to the fullness of discipleship. It remains a scandal to many that even now we are not afforded the rights and respect men in church and society take for granted. Yet, from what I have found, nothing — neither domination nor subordination, neither abuse nor condescension — can squelch the life of the spirit women seek to live.

"Womanspirit" offsets pomposity by humor. Witness the gentle-as-a-dove, wise-as-a-serpent way in which "womanspirit" rises in the face of challenge. Catherine of Siena, named a doctor of the church, became a counselor to popes at a time when women were banned from the inner circles of ecclesiastical politics, and Teresa of Avila, the only other woman accorded the same title, submitted her writings to church authorities while managing to sidestep the Spanish inquisitors.

Closer to home we witness women's pioneering spirit in the history of our country — their courage to tend homesteads, to bear and raise children under horrendous conditions, to overcome disease, death, and desertion. Compassion for the poor and uneducated, a willingness to shelter strangers, an offer to care for the ill and elderly, tasks dismissed by men as "women's work," were not refused. Women are the foundresses of thousands of missions, schools, homes, and hospitals. Women people the fields of law, medicine, business, politics, and education. We excel in the arts and sciences. The proverbial put-down, "She's only a woman, and women don't do these things," is put to rest by the words of a truer saying, "A man's work is from sun to sun, but a woman's work is never done."

The more I thought, listened, and read, the more I realized that this book would have to organize itself around a number of motifs recurrent in women's self-reflection. While I wrote the book, it was as if the book began to write itself through me. One motif was memory. Women have an amazing capacity to remember. While my sprightly mother, now in her eighties, may not be able to recall what she had for breakfast, she can remember everything that happened to her as she pursued a career in retailing at a time when Italian women were supposed to "stay barefoot in the kitchen and raise bambinos."

Women know their history personally and collectively, biblically and secularly. Women believe there is truth in the telling of a story. That's what makes writers like Flannery O'Connor, Alice Walker, Annie Dillard, and Toni Morrison so great. Women imagine what the world might look like if people learned to love one another, to remove diminishing stereotypes, and to propose ways of thinking that would foster reform in church and society. To listen without judging, to take risks without killing originality — these are essential starting points as we enter a new era of faith and creativity, of friendship and mutuality.

Women are good at what we do from homemaking and mothering to monitoring careers. Women take credit for what we accomplish, but status and success are no longer seen as sufficient sources of happiness. Other, more important aims of life are loving and trusting, befriending and bonding, connecting and networking. Sin and selfishness do block the vision we behold of what can be. Envy and jealousy prevail over the celebration of gifts. Defenses diminish the development of relationships. Such is the human condition, and so, too, is the call for renewal.

Women are not afraid to probe their feelings. We welcome being in relationships that draw forth our anger at unjust treatment and our desire for amiability. Emotions are as essential to us as ideas. We care about the way in which we and others are growing alone and together. We are comfortable sharing what happens to us when we pray and play. Like Julian of Norwich, we are not embarrassed to share our "showings" of the Most High. We accept that life can be as simple as smelling the roses, as risky as falling in love.

Women are beginning to appreciate the gifts God gives us, whatever our age, color, or creed may be. Any split between body and spirit, mind and matter, reason and faith is rejected. We see ourselves as sexual-spiritual, affective-cognitive, intuitive-intelligent human beings.

The formation theory of personality initiated by Adrian van Kaam, upon which I draw amply in this book, has immense appeal in this regard. Women think with heads and hearts in crisis moments and in periods of relative calm. We are at once vital, functional, and transcendent. We are fully alive persons in our own right, not merely the "other half" of the human race.

"Peace," "joy," "healing," "wholeness" are frequent words in women's vocabulary. I wish it were within my power as a writer to mine the depths of our collective experience but, even now, at this book's end the story continues. I do understand more about myself, God, and the church, but each disclosure reveals a path still concealed from view. How, after all, does one hold a rainbow in her hand? I believe that somewhere over this brightly colored bridge there is a pot of gold. The treasure I anticipate finding is that women in church and society refuse to give up hope. This disposition springs eternal, like the tent city that arose in the ruins of the 1989 earthquake in Santa Cruz, tagged by residents the "Phoenix Mall."

Hope is the virtue I most associate with a person's being touched by the hand of God. It is a lifespring that no holocaust or hypocrisy can hold down. Even in the face of failed expectations and unnecessary defeats, women carry themselves and the church forward to a new tomorrow. Such hope humbles me.

Women's faith in God, in life, in the future enables us to pass through and beyond painful times of transition to a new era of progress modeled on nothing less than the loving exchanges between Jesus and women, the depths of which have yet to be explored.

1

For to be a woman is to have interests and duties, ranging out in all directions from the central mother-core, like spokes from the hub of a wheel. The pattern of our lives is essentially circular.
— *Anne Morrow Lindbergh*

Who Is Woman?

Hey little girl,
Where have you been?

Hey little girl,
Where will you go?

Hey little girl?
Why are you sad?

Hey little girl,
Here is your beau.

— A child's playtime verse

We do not consider talking together over lunch for three hours a waste of time.
— Two Mennonite women

I am woman...I am...a child of God, full of grace and dignity...I am God's beloved, unique and free to form friendships, to marry or to stay single, depending on my life call....What, then, inclines others to label me? To frame my life in their design? To make me a victim of oppressive structures, attitudinal prejudices, crass stereotypes? Power and subjugation overshadow equality and respect as if I, woman, were a thing to be used, an object to be traded, a commodity to create pleasure.

I am woman...I am...many tongues rejoicing, many crying in pain...I am yellow, brown, black, red, and white....I am a multitude of cultures and creeds, talents and gifts. I am an Edith Stein, inspiring the world to hope in the face of despair; a Mother Teresa of Calcutta, beholding life in people dying and dismissed as untouchable; a Louise de Marillac offering charity and healing to the poor and sick of the earth; a Thea Bowman, preaching wherever God places her.

My name is known and unknown. I am called the "Samaritan woman," yet the Lord God himself sat and spoke with me. Once I understood what it meant to worship in spirit and truth, I gladly gathered the people to him (Jn. 4:7–42). I am Mary of Bethany, Jesus' friend, of whom he said I chose the better part (Lk. 10:38–42). Would you have done any less than sit in quiet awe in his presence had you been there? I am Mary Magdalene, the woman to whom he gave the great privilege of announcing — imagine my joy! — that he, whom I saw buried, was truly risen as he said (Mt. 28:1–10). I am the Canaanite woman, full of faith, whose persistence the Master could not resist (Mt. 15:21–28).

I am she whom you know . . . an inspiration to many, a teller of tales full of mercy and misery, miracles and menace. . . . Not for me are analysis and abstraction alone. I like it best when thoughts and feelings, ideas and emotions blend like the ingredients of a fine stew, or when swirls of oil subtly brushed on canvas produce a portrait exactly like the real person. The story I am about to tell you is true.

> In 1960 a North Vietnamese 122-mm rocket sailed in over Saigon — a Soviet-made rocket with about a fifty-pound warhead — toward the old Saigon Basilica. Directly in front of this edifice stood a tall, stately, snow-white statue of the Virgin — on a small, slightly raised dais of earth with at that time a concrete border and retainer.
>
> The rocket missed the basilica (and judging from the angle of its entry into the ground must just barely have missed the superstructure of the cathedral) and almost, *but not quite*, hit the beautiful statue. Its detonation blasted a very large crater directly behind the Virgin (who continued to gaze out serenely over Saigon, as if to indicate that nothing of lasting importance had happened here).
>
> I arrived on the scene only minutes after the impact, having felt its vibrations through my bones — and found the

deep crater behind the Virgin exuding gray smoke (as if it were a side-entrance to hell itself) — but there stood the unmoved Blessed Virgin, regal, beneficent, kindly, motherly, gazing out onto a city lost in war, but not lost, apparently, to her eye, or to her beatific understanding.

— From the author, Ted Lechner,
in a letter to my friend, S.R.

I, woman, witness suffering around family tables as well as in war zones. I weep with mothers everywhere whose children are lost. Strange, isn't it? Men make war over boundaries whereas women want to cross them. . . . I want us to dance in unison, not to tear one another apart.

I believe in body and mind, in sense and spirit, working together. I live in the rhythms of privacy and community, silence and speech, abiding and action. At times women can do something to make life better. At other times all we can do is wait. . . .

During the month of June, I . . . was privileged to spend about eight days at various times with my best friend who had been gradually dying over the last three years from an extremely rare liver disease, cause unknown. This friend and her family had lived with my family for close to two years. We were closer than sisters and we could truly share our hearts with one another. Having lived together we knew the best and the worst of one another, our strengths and weaknesses.

Four days before she died, I and another friend who had also lived with M. in community felt we were to go to the university hospital to see her. It was the last time we saw her in this life. She was the color of an orange, extremely weak and constantly thirsty as she was on a limited fluid intake. Yet what exuded from her was gratitude and appreciation for life and all its gifts and faith in God's goodness. The three of us cried together, laughed together, and A. and I and her sister took turns doing what little things we could for her.

At one point I leaned over M. to swab her lips with a . . . pink sponge and I was hit with almost a visceral reaction — "My God, she's drying out just like Jesus on the cross that Julian [of Norwich] saw," was the thought that pierced me. And in my mind I saw the silhouettes of Mary and John at the foot of the cross totally helpless to do anything... then it [this same image] flipped to M. drying out on the cross — to M. being Christ and that somehow A. and I had been privileged to do for Christ what Mary and John and the others would have done....

> — From the account of a "formation event"
> written by J. J., a student at Duquesne University

I, woman, made in the form and likeness of God, equal in dignity to every other human person, have been cruelly discriminated against because of my sex. I have been called temptress, playmate, viper by men who have forgotten the words of Pope John XXIII that "... women will not tolerate being treated as mere material instruments, but demand rights befitting a human person both in domestic and public life."

Some may find my words abrasive, but there is cause. I have been denied the right and freedom to choose whom to marry, to embrace a single life were that my calling, to obtain an education, to take part in decision making that directly affects me and my children.

> I was fifteen when I first asked my father if I could go to college. I mustered the courage to enter his barber shop when I saw that he wasn't too busy. I thought it would be better to ask him such a question in public. After all I wanted in the worse way to be a lawyer. So I said there in front of everybody, "Pop, I want to go to college someday soon, o.k.?" He slapped me hard, right across the face. No one said anything. "There's your school," he answered. I went back to work at the five-and-ten store. Later I did well in the retail business. I never forgot that slap, and I still want to be a lawyer.
>
> — My mother at eighty

I, woman, am a victim but, as history shows, I am more often than not a survivor. I know what it is to bear responsibility with or without the rewards. I've crossed prairies by wagon train, given birth in open fields, fought for the right to vote and hold public office, insisted on due process and the laws of affirmative action. I teach, legislate, and act decisively. I parent daughters and sons on my own, while not receiving comparable pay for comparable work. I am treated as a second-class citizen, not afforded the chance

to use my gifts to the full in church and society — and still I find
time to sing and pray, to tell stories to children, to break bread with
strangers, to do what has to be done. It is not an easy life, but it
has its moments.

> You can't always change things. Sometimes you don't have
> no control over the way things go. Hail ruins the crops or
> fire burns you out. And then you're just given so much to
> work with in a life and you have to do the best you can
> with what you got. That's what piecing is. The materials is
> passed on to you or is all you can afford to buy . . . that's just
> what's given to you. Your fate. But the way you put them
> together is your business. You can put them in any order
> you like. Piecing is orderly. First you cut the pieces, then you
> arrange your pieces just like you want them. I build up the
> blocks and then put all the blocks together and arrange them,
> then I strip and post to hold them together . . . and finally I
> bind them all around and you got the whole thing made up.
> Finished.
>
> — Mary, a quilter, in *The Quilters:*
> *Women and Domestic Art, An Oral History*

The story of woman continues because God's chosen ones,
followers of Jesus, the Liberator, have not yet put on heartfelt compassion, kindness, humility, gentleness, and patience. We batter
rather than bear with one another. Getting even takes precedence
over forgiving faults — and when shall we put on love (Col. 3:12–
14)? When shall we behave as if we really are one in Christ Jesus
(Gal. 3:28)?

Even I, woman, wellspring of life and love, have been reduced
to hate. I, too, have taken up the gun and the sword. And when
the young lie dying, I wonder if there ever is a righteous cause for
killing. War is loud. Then the cries and clamor fall silent and the
battlefield is strewn with blood. Even quiet, chemical wars end in
death, and we all lie dying.

I, homeless woman, am asleep in an open doorway, leaning cold
against my bag of rags. When I was but a child I became pregnant.
My lover didn't want the baby. It died at the clinic and so did I, a
little. . . . I, young woman, prostitute myself to satisfy the addiction
that enslaves me. I, old woman, once so pretty, am wrinkled, alone,
and poor. I sit in my own wetness in a home that isn't a home at

all. I hope, maybe, that God still loves me, a little.... Ah, woman, fear not — you are loved, a lot! You are woman.... You are a child of God, full of grace and dignity.... You are God's beloved, unique and free.... You are wise and whole and holy. You are your story, and the telling is only beginning.

2

A Christian Woman Remembers: Childhood

THE ROAR OF NIAGARA FALLS, powerful, rushing, pulsating, is the first sound I remember. When I was three years old, my mother took me for walks in the park near the small apartment where we lived in the post-war years, while my father completed an assignment at the naval shipping yards, adjacent to this wonder of the world.

Growing up in an Italian Catholic family has its blessings as well as its drawbacks. From the point of view of religious upbringing, I was lucky. The atmosphere was more relaxed than rigid. God's mercy to sinners was more important than minute adherence to moral codes. I did not suffer from any Jansenistic despisal of matter. The difference between my own character formation and that of an Irish Catholic friend's became clear when he told me that the main source of tension around his dinner table stemmed from the quality of the conversation while for me the center of interest was and remains the flavor of the food.

Doctrines and dogmas notwithstanding, the main test of Christian living was the love shown to one's family and friends. Touching was as acceptable an expression of affection as telling a story. The issue I had to deal with was not alienation from my sexuality but potential estrangement from my inmost life call due to familial expectations.

The same heritage that sustains life through food and warmth was marked by a tendency to both overdirect and overprotect its children. The "mama and papa know best" rule of thumb hampered emotional maturity. I am not the first and certainly I will not be the last woman to feel overpowered by a well intended love that does not know when to let go and give a budding self room to grow.

My quest to be as free as the flowing waters of the Falls — while framed in by responsible borders — continues to this day. I've been told, better too much love than not enough, and that seems true when one considers the deforming effects of love withheld or abused. Perhaps it is impossible to achieve the right balance between children's needs and parents' attempts to meet them.

My mother and I have a lot in common and still do — an aesthetic taste, an interest in art, a love for order, a flair for cooking — but we are also unique women. This latter lesson requires a lot of learning on both sides. Here, too, there is truth in the saying that the older we get, the wiser our elders become.

I remember being a naturally devout child, open to a mystery beyond myself while being somewhat hesitant to form proximate relationships. I masked my shyness by a brave front of independence, a trait that would lead later to unnecessary loneliness. This tendency to draw inward lasted through my teenage years. It was hard to admit, even harder to overcome. I defended my sensitivity by taking distance from others, preferring to bury myself in books rather than to be exposed to painful scrutiny by my peers, brothers, and parents.

On the lighter side, I enjoyed childish pranks, had a good sense of humor, and was liked by my playmates for the original games I invented. Still waters that run deep often kept me slightly apart. I was actually a kindergarten drop-out — ostensibly because Miss M. was mean and ugly as a witch. The real reason was again rooted in fear of her power over me and my own sense of inadequacy. I was simply not yet ready to face the world.

Once I got to first grade, I was fine, mainly because of a woman. My first grade teacher, Sister Gemma, was a gentle, loving soul, a real "gem," who instilled in me a sense of being cared for by God, who loved us like a mother. God's love was not overpowering but empowering. Of course, my vocabulary did not include such words. I know now that they describe the discovery that God's love creates space for grace; it is freeing, not coercive; it is utterly unconditional.

Christ's presence shone through this woman's whole being. She was the same in and out of the classroom. In those days, we learned about God from the Baltimore catechism, but we came to know God through Sister Gemma. Her counsel to us came down to three words: "Talk to God." When we cried because we were too embarrassed to speak, she would say, "There, there, now, you'll be fine. Just talk your troubles over with God." When we got into arguments with parents and peers, the counsel was the same, "Remember to talk over what's bothering you with God; then you'll see how easy it is to talk to one another." Thanks to Sister Gemma, I know to this day that there is nothing I cannot talk over with God. Later in life I came across Teresa of Avila's definition of prayer as an intimate conversation with the God who loves us. I already knew that was true from the phrase imprinted on my heart by a sister who kept the channels of communication open by telling us a thousand times over that it was always time to talk to God. It was the same as talking to a friend.

Learning came easy to me. Making good grades was not a problem. What caused me the most joy and the most pain were not report cards but those ever elusive familial and social relationships. I was still too young to realize the "for better or worse" nature of family life. We all want to remember our beginnings through rose-colored glasses. The truth is that for every ounce of good formation, instances of deformation occur unwittingly. For every successful social encounter, there is at least one counterbalancing incident of trust betrayed. I wish I had a record of the number of "best friends" that entered and exited the stage of my adolescent years. I can count on a few fingers the contacts that have lasted. I realize that many women and men who read this book still enjoy high school, even grade school, reunions where forever bonds were formed, but such has not been my experience. To be a friend to others we must first, in a way, befriend ourselves, and, on the score of "know and love thyself," I had many more lessons to learn.

Getting back to first grade, Sister Gemma continued to remind us to talk to Jesus about everything. "Tell Jesus about your friends and your enemies, about your progress in school, your relationships with your family, your times of work and play. He likes to hear all you have to say." Her words went straight to my heart.

We also heard volumes about the communion of saints. They were our Catholic heros and heroines. Sister advised us — as if the parties in question were sipping tea in the next room attentive to our communications — to call upon Lucy for eye trouble, Blaise for throat pain, Jude for impossible causes, Christopher for safety on the road, Anthony for things lost that could not be found. Last but not least, we could count on our namesake (in my case, Susanna) when we needed a special line to heaven. No doubt the conduit for these many petitions was the guardian angel who hovered near us when we were good and protected us "more than we would ever know" from harm. Does this kind of Catholic upbringing still exist, or has it descended into the murky depths of mythological lore?

When I was ten years old and just starting to wonder about the "facts of life," I had a rare opportunity to learn them, not in a sex education class but at home. My mother, who was forty-two at the time, brought me into her bedroom. She closed the door, and we sat in silence for a while. It was a winter day, but the sun shone brightly through the window panes. I asked her what was the matter. She said: "Nothing and everything. I'm going to have a baby in September. I didn't think I could have any more children." It was stunning news! I was ten, my brother, eight, my father, forty-eight. We all thought our family was complete, and now this! On that unforgettable morning, Mother answered the questions I had secretly formulated but never voiced. All I could do after our frank discussion was place my hands on her stomach and assure her not to be afraid. Everything would be fine. Then we cried and laughed at the same time. We shared a mother-daughter moment of intimacy as wonderful as any I have ever known. It was as if we were standing together on the edge of life's deepest mystery. Two years later, at the age of twelve, I had an equally jarring experience of death.

I had been told for some time that my maternal grandmother's stomach cancer was terminal, but the finality of that word had not fully registered. I clung to the belief that she would recover, that I would feel her arms hugging me once more, that I would inhale the life-giving, freshly-baked-bread scent of her body and bask in the lilt of her infectious laughter. I wanted to feel warmed again by the winks of wisdom reserved for me alone. I knew I was the grandchild she favored most because with me she could share without words the depth of her Catholic faith. Now the light was growing dim. Nothing, not even the full force of my love, could hold back the dark.

The night that she died — this uneducated, illiterate, peasant woman, who mothered eleven children, who was a paragon of virtue, whose Christian witness I shall never forget — that night I could not weep. The tears came, wetting my face like the rain for which she, with her "green thumb," always praised God, only on the day she was buried, not once during the funeral. It took time to work through my childish anger at God, to accept that death snatches those we love without asking our permission.

On the evening of her passing (was it to forestall my mourning?), my godmother, a beautician by trade, took me in the bathroom and said she was going to cut my hair. I offered no resistance. I had long brown tresses that had only been trimmed, never shorn. I allowed her to clip away until the hair curled around my ears. When my mother saw what she had done, she went into hysterics, but it was too late. My hair lay in piles on the rug. Maybe those shorn tresses symbolized the loss I could not voice due to my beloved grandmother's departure. Just as there was no way of putting those hairs back on my head, so there was no way of bringing her back from the dead.

My grandmother accepted God's plan for her life in the face of almost insurmountable odds. Having witnessed the depths of her faith, its power to sustain her throughout an excruciating illness, I could no long deny that there might be a divine design for my life too. Because "nunny" trusted God's love, even when she was alone and in pain, I would too. At the age of sixteen, she had been transported by steamer from southern Italy to America to marry a man she had met only briefly through a matchmaker. Of her eleven children, five died before puberty, some in childbirth. There were few times of peace and prosperity during her seventy-two years, but she never complained; she never betrayed her faith. In her heart she believed God had reasons that reason itself would never understand. My resolutions to emulate her were no bigger than mustard seeds, but her life remains the remembered soil in which my faith continues to grow.

A few months after this loss, as an indicator, no doubt, of the slow-as-a-turtle pace of my spiritual progress, I had my first major fight with God. During one of the many hours I spent alone in my room daydreaming, reading, just missing her, I began voicing a vague promise to live my life in tune with the forming power on which "nunny" based her faith. What I was not prepared to accept were the demands such an assent might mean. Though I played it cool with the other girls in the eighth grade, I knew inside that I was different, if nothing else, more reflective — a tendency I strove mightily to hide. So I giggled, even if I did not find the boys' jokes particularly funny. I confessed to the girls' room crowd my first crush on E., an acknowledged "totally cool" guy, who wore a black leather jacket and once walked me home from school. I was considered a bit of a "brain," and even without trying I still received a few "highest marks" in literature and social studies. On the surface I was pretty popular but inside I knew I was being prompted to another level of awareness. But of what? Of whom? I wondered if others my age ever thought as much about things like life and death as I did. Answers were not to be found in attending religion classes nor did I feel at all attracted to the convent as a few of the girls in my Catholic school did.

One day I decided to have it out with God. I vented my anger and confusion. I wanted God to answer the great questions or to leave me alone. I wanted out of the pact I had made at the time of grandmother's death, the promise to be faithful — whatever that might mean. I was suffering from a feeling of inner solitude, pretending to conform to peer notions of fun when I really felt fragmented. I was conscious of being beckoned to I knew not where, and I was afraid.

I remember walking to the end of our yard and begging God to leave me alone, to let me be like everyone else. I did not want to take the road less traveled or dance to a different drummer. When the venting ceased, I felt drained of emotion but strangely at peace. It was as if God had confirmed my feelings by allowing me to be exactly who and where I was.

The meaning of these two events, "nunny's" death and the backyard bout, have never left me. They form an integral part of my Christian childhood, and in one way or another disclosed a pattern in my life of prayer. When I am at my lowest ebb, and yet perfectly honest with God, the gloom lessens and a new direction is delicately disclosed. Bits and pieces of my early and later formation gather around the seminal events of birth and death, beginnings and ends, goals reached and uncharted terrain yet to traverse.

Another memory, this one linked to a penchant for ministry, comes to mind in relation to my father. Like many Italian men, he thought regular church-going was mainly for women. For the longest time I didn't say anything about our going to Mass on Sunday without him. Then, not long after grandmother's death, fired by the desire to keep alive the flame of her faith commitment, I decided that my first mission would be to get my father to go to Mass regularly.

My tactics were hardly subtle. I began my campaign by lecturing him on the value of attending Mass every Sunday, not merely on feast days like Christmas and Easter. This approach succeeded only in cementing his stubbornness. He had his own way with God and I was entitled to mine. Knowing I had reached an impasse with the lecture route, I tried to shame him into attendance, appearing on Sunday morning in church garb, missal in hand, refusing even water to keep the fast, and saying, when he would offer to drive me, that I preferred to walk. Self-righteous faith never produces good fruit, as I soon found out. Dad refused to broach the subject, and, as a newly self-commissioned missionary, I dubbed my ministry a failure.

One Sunday I arose earlier than usual. Mother was already in the kitchen while Dad was lying in bed reading the paper. I stood in the doorway of his room. He looked up with eyes that told me he did not want another lecture. Tears began streaming down my face. I said I only wanted to be in church with him. If he chose not to go, then neither would I. We looked at each other for a long time like two stubborn Italians. Then he told me sternly to go and get dressed. I saw him turn back to the paper and concluded that his heart must be hard as stone and I had no way to crack it. So much for trusting in grace.

When I came downstairs a short while later, I saw Mother smiling while not saying a word. I could hear Dad in the bathroom singing and shaving. He came out, nicely dressed, finished his toast and coffee, glanced at his watch and casually said, "Isn't it almost time for Mass?" From that Sunday onward, he seldom missed. I sensed then spiritual truths God has confirmed over and over. When we get our ego plans out of the way, God has room to work; when we witness to faith, instead of preaching about it, people will respond in ways beyond our expectations; when we offer another person love, love is enkindled in turn.

The reverse comes to memory in the guise of a mean teacher, one of the few I encountered in my early education. One day my "crush," whom she obviously hated because he was considered a leader by the class, answered her orders about keeping our lockers cleaned with the smart-mouth remark, "We ain't here to be janitors." Wrong move. Her fury came forth like a suddenly raging tropical storm. With a menacing frown, through pinched white lips, she marched the entire class into the hall and lined us up on the left-hand side. At least five lockers on the right of the hallway were slightly ajar. In front of everyone she grabbed this boy by the neck of his jersey and proceeded to smash his back against each of those lockers, shocking him speechless in the process. When she finished closing the entire wall of lockers with his bruised back, she hurled him into the line. We watched her display of temper and power in utter disbelief. Taller and stronger than anyone there, she croaked that if we insulted her intelligence again, we would be punished even more severely. Complaints were of no use in those days. We simply had to await her transfer, which mercifully occurred the following semester.

Soon after this ghastly event we had to prepare for confirmation. Prior to the reception of the sacrament, it was customary to choose a confirmation name. The one I took was "Veronica" in memory of the woman who wiped the face of Jesus as he walked the way of the cross to Golgotha. Little is known about her — only this one act of compassion. What she did seemed to me so spontaneous, so kind. For some reason I could identify with her courage to console Christ as his energy ebbed under the weight of the wood. I imagined what it would have been like to be there: the shouts, the sweat, the stripping away of his dignity with each lash of the whip. How wonderful it would have been to break through the ranks of hateful vengeance and reveal in one bold gesture how much I cared; to wipe his face and let him feel at this moment of utter isolation a bit less despised; to show him that he had at least one loving friend among those who told his captors to complete the crucifixion.

Veronica's reaching out to touch Christ and his welcoming of this intimate contact spoke to me of the divine friendship I sought to receive through the sacrament of confirmation. This new name made me feel as if Veronica and I were one in our desire to do God's will. This desire welled up with great power several years later when I knelt, wept, and prayed at the foot of a cross hung on my apartment wall. Having betrayed the "grand design," I begged God to shadow me once again under the protective "wings" of the divine presence. Having tuned *out* for a while, having experienced devastating unhappiness, I knew without a doubt that I could only be happy if I tuned *in* to that holy plan, not as a puppet but as a person ready and willing to follow the adventure providence had in store.

The end of elementary school marked the end of childhood, the beginning of adolescence. I entered a coed Catholic high school, met a new group of friends, gravitated toward writing tasks like editing the yearbook and the school paper. While I enjoyed a fair degree of popularity, I also experienced a gnawing sense of solitude. Over the next four years, I felt keenly at times the "difference factor" I could never quite dismiss. I continued asking of God the key question: what would you have me do? For the longest time I did not listen. There was the surface me and the private me: the girl with leadership and verbal gifts, and the young woman who felt touched by "I don't know what." Weak of spirit, I was yet determined to respond affirmatively, whatever that might mean.

I identified with another young woman, Anne Frank, whose *Diary of a Young Girl* became a dear companion. Anne, too, lived under the canopy of "doubleness": the Anne people saw, bubbling, energetic, creative, and the Anne only "Kitty," her diary, knew. She had to endure enforced solitude and the chilling forecast of captivity by the Nazis. All the while she and the others were hiding, the little chatterbox, as she was called, brought to an otherwise gloomy attic existence a degree of lightheartedness and hope. For a girl her age, she had a remarkable spirituality, not unlike that of Thérèse of Lisieux. On the eve of her capture and subsequent execution, Anne expressed her belief that people, however cruel they might appear, were really good at heart. Not even the holocaust can snuff out the light of God's love.

The seeds of faith and fidelity found in teachers, family members, friends, and books would not lie fallow. Planted in childhood, they would bloom in the field of spirituality that was to become my life's work. The way would seldom be smooth, but a strength greater than mine would make it straight. Life would unfold in a series of deaths, decisions, and rebirths. The journey begun in childhood would continue for years to come.

3   ❧

You know you're alive. You take huge steps, trying to feel the planet's roundness arc between your feet. Kazantzakis says that when he was young he had a canary and a globe. When he freed the canary, it would perch on the globe and sing. All his life, wandering the earth, he felt as though he had a canary on top of his mind, singing.

— *Annie Dillard*

A Christian Woman Remembers: Young Adulthood

*I*N HIGH SCHOOL as well as in college, I chose to remain a "commuter student." I lived at home, preferring the privacy of my own room to the clutter of a crowded dormitory. Coming to classes as I did from a distant neighborhood meant having to rely on public transportation — trolleys, buses, and occasionally the luxury of a taxicab. My high school was on the top of Mount Washington overlooking the city of Pittsburgh in the days when it seemed to be dark at noon, so dense was the air pollution from steel mills operating around the clock. Change came slowly, but from my freshman to my senior year, the view from the top became justifiably famous.

Those trolley rides in all seasons honed my powers of observation. I already had dreams of being a journalist. Life had lessons to teach I could never learn from books. To be a writer was a vocation that intrigued me from as far back as I could remember. I felt sure that one's senses had to be fine tuned for writing to succeed. I had to learn to see, hear, smell, taste, and touch with my pen.

Nothing fascinated me more than finding the right words to describe the sight of a distant star or a snatch of conversation overheard on one of my trolley runs: " ... that was when I turned and ran as fast as I could. ... " From what? From whom? A dog, a jealous lover, a bolt of lightning? "And then she had the nerve to say. ... "

30

Who? A relative, a teacher, a friend? And what? That you were a liar, wore an ugly dress, flirted with her husband? These word games passed the time while teaching me to think imaginatively.

If I intended to master the art of writing, I knew I had to become a disciple of words — their power, beauty, and variability, their music, rhythm, and sound. While I could hardly wait to get to my composition class, I had to force myself into the chemistry lab. My heart pounded with recognition when I read journals like Henry David Thoreau's *Walden*. Sheer observation told me that the mass of men does lead lives of quiet desperation, but he said it. I saw their faces every morning on the way to school. I felt sorry for their lack of spirit. I wanted to help, but how? I absorbed with love the poetry of that reclusive wit, Emily Dickinson. How right she was when she wrote that much madness is divinest sense to the discerning eye, much sense the starkest madness.

How could one compare this wondrous choice of just the right word with something as bland as the formula for water or sodium? Miraculous as these numbers and letters might be to another type of mind, I preferred words that said what something sounded like: squish... or what it felt like: ooze... or how it alliterated alluringly, sounded as exotic as Singapore, as erotic as the South Seas on a sultry, summer day, as ecstatic as a spirit drawn from mundane matter to the mystery of divine mercy. How could one harness the power propelling words from the dull to the dynamic? Writing was work, but the results, when good, were enough reward.

I discovered during those morning and afternoon commutes that I not only enjoyed people watching; I could also read whatever my eyes alighted on from a textbook or a novel to ad copy or road signs. Between my freshman and sophomore year, my first real summer job happened to be in the advertising department of a toy manufacturing company in downtown Pittsburgh. I soon discovered that I had not wasted time on those long trolley runs. The supervisor asked me one morning to suggest some ideas for promoting a new gadget. I felt flattered. Here I was "toying" with the idea of becoming a journalist and now I had the chance to practice advertising on an amateur basis. I must add that I was working with a woman, perhaps twice my age, who was supposed to teach me how to process the orders. She did so minimally and reluctantly. I did not complain because I caught on quickly to the system and seemed to make a good impression on our supervisor. When he asked for my input, I dashed something off from the top of my head without giving it a second thought — about a toy children would have a tough time keeping because it was something their parents would want to play with too. "This is one thing that will bring out the child in you because it's never too late to play *Cool Pool*." Two days later my copy appeared in the local newspaper. The boss sent me a clipping, with a note of thanks and a few extra dollars in my paycheck. The thrill was short-lived because for the rest of the summer I had to endure the spiteful looks and snide remarks of my co-worker. She would not be won over, no matter what I said or did. As far as she was concerned, language skills were a curse, not a blessing.

Going to a Catholic school meant that we had annual retreats, regular religion classes, and ample opportunity for vocational counseling. I was both guided and misguided during these formative years. My surest guide was the inner conviction, already disclosed in childhood, that I had to be faithful to a call to "I knew not what," though in catechetical terms it was dubbed "God's will." What I had to avoid listening to were other voices like that of a visiting priest who said I should look into life in a religious community or that of a priest-counselor on the staff who was sure I belonged in a girls' college, majoring in secondary education. To make life more confusing, I had to appraise, in addition to these misdirections, the voices of bunches of relatives who were curious about my social life and the boys I was or was not dating. Added in were the taunts of peers who disliked my independent spirit and coaxed me to follow this or that clique, especially because of my position as editor of the yearbook.

There were at one time so many voices in my head that I had to stop listening to any of them. That was when I threw myself into activities with the energy of a caged lion: school newspaper, basketball team, drama group. I spent hours in the library, organized class picnics, took on other odd jobs. Unwittingly, I set myself on a course I would have to alter years later — escaping to the functional dimension of life when I should have paused, stepped aside, and had the courage to discern my direction candidly and courageously. Despite all the fun I was having at home and in school, many questions kept recurring: Which college should I attend? Did I like this boy enough to go with him? What did I know about dating compared with girls who had been going out since the age of twelve? Was I perhaps reading too much and getting fancy ideas into my head? The answers to these outer and inner questions seemed inadequate. For a long time I felt like the proverbial round peg in a square hole.

If I had expected such problems to be resolved by the time I was sixteen, I had a long wait ahead of me. That, by the way, was a birthday I shall never forget. My parents planned to take me to one of their favorite restaurants. One of my dad's friends, Phil, was the bartender. I felt like "hot stuff." I was learning to drive, I had on a new dress, my hair was a mass of dark curls, a boy I liked was the waiter, I mean, who could ask for anything more? My father invited me to sit and have a drink with him at the bar while we waited for my mother and brothers to arrive. I knew he had arranged for the kitchen to prepare a cake with sixteen candles and to send the waiters over to sing "Happy Birthday."

I slithered with as much sophistication as I could muster onto the bar stool and ordered, what else?, a "Manhattan." I thought about making it a "Martini," but somehow the "Big Apple" allure was hard to resist. My father raised his eyebrows, but nodded approval anyway when I said ever so softly to Phil, "Make mine a Manhattan." He winked knowingly and said, "Coming right up," three words that proved to be prophetic. Minutes later my head felt like a prune in a vise. Was this someone's idea of a good time? All I wanted to do was go to bed and hibernate like a bear for the duration of the winter, or maybe for the rest of my life. At least I kept my vow. That was the last time I ever said, "Make mine a Manhattan."

Another scene from this watershed year stays with me: the night of my junior prom. I was on a double date with a girl I thought I knew fairly well. My date was from another school. She was with a boy who had transferred to ours and whom she had been seeing off and on for a few months. I can still remember my chiffon dress — layer over layer of foam green ruffles billowing out around my feet like a swirl of seaweed on the ocean's floor. Hair fluffed, eyes shadowed in a matching hue, and the crowning glory of a lovely corsage from a tall shy boy, nervously adjusting the cuffs of his blue suit as he received my father's instructions about the best route to the gym and the time I had to be home. It was like a scene from a summer movie. If there are in this passing world one or two perfect moments, then I was surely in their midst.

Here was I, a late bloomer, to be sure, having hardly ever been kissed, strictly raised in an Italian Catholic family, saying good-bye to my parents, wearing a dreamy dress, on my way to the prom with a blond-haired, blue-eyed boy, who would have been the answer to any girl's prayers. I can still hear the beat of those '50s tunes, guiding the feet of two novice dancers who felt for all the world like Ginger Rogers and Fred Astaire. Though some of the guys and girls were drinking beer and smoking in the back alley, most of us were in the gym swilling nonalcoholic punch and munching finger sandwiches mounded on cafeteria trays, picking away at bowls of pretzels, laughing at nothing and everything. The smell of honest sweat mingled with the pungency of a hundred different perfumes and aftershave lotions was enough to make anyone lightheaded.

I had seen my girlfriend off and on during the dance, but someone in the girl's room said, when I could not find her, that she was in the back seat of the car "making out." I said that was ridiculous, left the bathroom, and went back to the gym. The band played until eleven, then one more song for an encore. Off we went. Everyone planned to meet at a restaurant overlooking the city for a midnight snack. I had permission to stay out until 1:00 A.M. We got to the car only to find the doors already open. I knew in a glance that what the other girls had told me was true. My friend and her date had left the dance early. One look at her disheveled state was enough to make me blush from ear to ear. Whatever she had experienced for the past hour was in such contrast to what I thought this night was about that I could not speak. My date and hers exchanged knowing glances. Either I was being sized up as a party-pooper or she as a good-time girl. Whatever the conclusion, I knew my balloon had burst. This lack of care for me or my feelings on the part of a person whom I had trusted drew the evening to sudden closure on a sour note.

What I experienced that evening was not clear until many years later. It had something to do with life choices, with keeping my integrity and recognizing that there had to be more to growing up than being "popular." I guess my grandmother knew what she was talking about when she said you have to eat a ton of salt with a person before you really know them. Even so, friendship will always involve a risk.

I went on to graduate with honors, entered Duquesne University, became editor of our college newspaper and chose to double major in English and journalism. During my college years, President John F. Kennedy was assassinated and so was Martin Luther King. Everything began to go crazy with all that the 1960s came to represent from Woodstock to Vietnam War protests. I immersed myself in study, taking a variety of elective courses in philosophy, theology, and psychology in addition to the required curriculum. Little did I know at the time that these discipline-related fields would provide the background I needed to understand and contribute to the theoretical-integrative approach of formative spirituality. Nor could I have foreseen that a set of providential circumstances would lead me back to Duquesne a few years after graduation to begin the next twenty plus years of my life as a teacher and administrator in the institute founded by Father Adrian van Kaam, the initiator of formation science with whom I would eventually co-author several books.

College was still a time of intense direction appraisal for me. I enjoyed my social life but study came first. I knew how to relax with chips and beer, I joined a sorority, worked summers in my field and winters as a student aide, had a good social life, and learned what it meant to meet writing deadlines. I amassed an immense amount of head knowledge but came also to understand what it meant to know with the heart. There were times when I could not have survived the pressure without quiet moments alone in the chapel. As graduation neared and with it my long awaited youth hostel trip to Europe with the Modern Language Club, I watched many girlfriends' fingers shine with engagement rings. Mine was intentionally left bare. I simply could not imagine being married so soon. There was so much to see, to do, to learn. How could I spread my wings and manage a home at the same time? Others seemed capable of doing so, but not I. I even forsook the first job offer I received in favor of going back-packing for the entire summer from Copenhagen to Venice. It was in that city that someone I shall never forget saved my life.

Our American Youth Hostel tour had arrived in this most romantic of Italian cities. The sun shone brightly on St. Mark's Square. I had a sense of homecoming, hearing my language of origin, smelling the pungent odors with which I grew up, watching the women and men talk with their hands. Here in Venice we would slow the pace of travel and spend three and a half days in a hotel-hostel near the Square, with time to sun and swim at Lido

Beach. Evenings were unscheduled so we could stroll leisurely in and out of the many small cafés that lined the canals. I had a sense from the start that something wonderful would happen here.

On the orientation tour we always took with several other hostel groups I struck up a conversation with an English boy a few years older than I. Before returning to our various hotels, he and I agreed to meet the next afternoon at the beach. I was sure I had fallen in love. Was it Venice? Was it his charming accent or the fact that he could carry on a stimulating conversation with feeling and intelligence without saying "Wow!" or "Gee whiz!" Was what I felt due to being in Europe, free from the strictures of youth, in love with the idea of love? Or could this wondrous feeling, this heady sensation, this romantic "high" be a signal of the "real thing"? I had had my share of crushes, but no prior experience could compare to this whirl of emotions. My traveling companions could not resonate with what I saw in him. They only wished they could find someone who made them feel that way.

Waiting for the next day to come took forever. At last I was on the beach. I did not see my new friend at first. Then he came up from behind, surprised me, and we started to laugh. We picked up the conversation we were engaged in the day before with the same animation. He was studying architecture in England. I told him I intended to begin studies for my master's degree in English literature at the University of Pittsburgh in the fall. This was his second time in Venice. He hoped to come every year, would I? If only that were possible, but.... We shared stories of childhood, of experiences at school, even religious affiliations, for, though not a Catholic, he was a committed Christian. He, too, knew what it felt like to be alone, to want something more out of life than a mere nine to five routine, to walk to the tune of a different drummer.

After about two hours of nonstop banter, I said I wanted to go for a swim as far as the sand bar. He wanted to lie in the sun for a while and think of our talk, but he would follow soon. I went into the water, by this time overheated from the temperature outside and the rise of several degrees within. I felt so happy, so carefree. I could have stayed in Italy permanently, with no past, no future, only the present. I was swimming along leisurely, the water by now well over my head. There was a slight undertow, but nothing alarming. Suddenly, without warning, I got a severe leg cramp. Not being the best of swimmers, I started to panic, waving my arms and spontaneously shouting his name. I kept trying to touch the sand bar with my toe, went under twice, gasped for air, tried to tread water, and then really became tight. No one seemed to be around. I was almost out of breath. I shouted once more. I took in two mouthfuls of water. I tried to turn over and float but began shaking uncontrollably. All of this took place in perhaps sixty to ninety seconds. Then I felt his arms around my waist pulling me swiftly along to the sand bar. I started to cry. I clung to him, saying between sobs that he had saved my life. He was gentle, soothing. He assured me he had heard my call immediately. I had been in no danger, but he could understand how frightened I felt. He rubbed the cramp out and, when I relaxed, he swam next to me, slowly and steadily back to shore.

That night we separated from our groups and celebrated together. We ate in a candlelit cafe, watched the fireworks commemorating a local holiday, and arranged to meet again in London when my tour group got there a few weeks later. He wanted me to stay in England with him, maybe study at Oxford or Cambridge. We could live together and see what would happen after that. I wanted to say yes with all my heart, but I could not dismiss the other voice calling me home. Saying good-bye was as difficult for him as it was for me. Had I stepped out of a novel, the scene could not have been more poignant. We wrote for months thereafter. I hoped he would come to the States, but life directions and decisions intervened and we drifted apart. He has a special place in my heart in this story of youth remembered, not only because of the gentle man he was but because I believe that God put him in that sea when I needed to be saved, and I believe that God granted me through this brief but intense encounter a glimpse of my womanhood.

I matured considerably that summer, strengthened by experience, convinced that I was truly loveable, and more than ever committed to remaining open to God's guiding of my life. Two years later I was led to what would turn out to be a lifelong ministry in lay formation. Marriage was not in the offing, but friendships proved to be as great a gift. I made a career shift from journalism to teaching literature and spirituality, kept my hand in editing by organizing two journals published by our Institute of Man, and went on to complete my doctorate in the literature of post-Reformation spirituality. In due course I published the first of several books on spiritual reading and on various disciplines and dispositions relevant to the life of the spirit. I learned with time to trust my call, though it would stretch me more than once to the limits. My ministry did not go together with any marriage offer I considered serious, so I chose to stay single, a vocation enabling me to remain open to the surprises of God and offering me the space I needed to be faithful to prior commitments.

When I was twenty-eight, I graduated from the University of Pittsburgh with my Ph.D. I began to develop courses in the literature of spirituality, evolving several years later into a six-semester cycle introducing graduate students to the classics of the Judaeo-Christian faith and formation tradition. I loved my work in the classroom as well as the administrative tasks to which I was appointed, culminating in the directorship of the institute from 1980 to 1988, the pioneering years of our own Ph.D. program in formative spirituality. To tell of my life during these years of helping Father Adrian van Kaam establish the new science of formation would require another book, one that he would be more qualified to write than I. What seems more to the point is to capture something of my own evolving spirit as a writer and a woman. Rather than relying on memory alone, I think the following letter to my father will explain better than anything I could write now what was occurring at this transition point from youth to maturing adulthood. I sent it to him a week before my birthday, on December 4, 1970:

> Dearest Dad:
>
> I think it is time to share with you where I am in my life and what my feelings are. I know that you share with me a sense of accomplishment at my being the first member of our family to receive a doctorate. Believe me when I say that you and Mom have played a special part in making this possible.
>
> I want to begin by saying that the doctorate is something I did in response to a deeper call. I love to study, to teach, to do research, and to write. Completing this work was not something motivated by a desire to make more money or to attain status. Both things are of secondary concern as perhaps what follows will make clear.
>
> When I say that I could not have completed this study without you and Mother behind me I mean this with all my heart. What really made the difference is that I knew both

of you would support me in my decisions and give me the freedom I needed to pursue them.

I also know that you, more so than Mother, are the all-time champion worrier. You care about your children and wonder if they are happy. You keep asking yourself, "Did I do enough? Did I say things that at times made them mad? Have I been a good father?" I know that you especially ask such questions in regard to me.

Let me say, Dad, that they are good questions and the answers hold nothing of which you have to be ashamed. They are a sign of your love, and they are appreciated. It is a great feeling to know that someone cares as much about me as you do. If I tell you not to worry about me, I know my words will be like peas bouncing off a wall because you'll worry anyway. But I guess what I need to say and what I hope you'll believe is that I am here and now a truly happy and grateful young woman. There are many reasons for my joy, and I want to share the most intimate with you.

The first is the sense of inner peace and freedom I feel knowing that my formal study is behind me and I am able to write without pressure. This happiness wells up from deep springs. It is related to the love I know you and Mother have for me, but it goes deeper still and is an expression of the love God has for all of us. I know God cares for me in a special way; this sustaining care is a source of inner contentment. God has given me you and Mother and two fine brothers. When I was an unhappy, mixed-up girl — realizing deep down that I could never make it in the dog-eat-dog world of journalism, when I prayed that I would find something meaningful to do, the Spirit led me to a wonderful ministry where I found the self I was meant to be. I discovered what it was like to work with students and colleagues whose dedication and sense of responsibility is refreshing in our self-centered world. I met in effect thousands of people who read the journals we edit, many of whom communicate in writing or in person an awareness of their own spiritual hunger.

Day after day my appreciation for this profession, that has, as it were, chosen me, increases as does my respect for Father Adrian's vision. I only hope that everything I do will be an expression of who I am. This applies not only to my writing and teaching, both of which I love, but to any chance I have to bring others some of the reasons I have for feeling so grateful.

Through writing, teaching, and public speaking, I believe I am helping others find answers to the questions we humans ask about life and death, joy and sorrow, pleasure and pain.

It is no wonder, then, that I thank God for all that has been given to me. When I look back over my life so far I can see a definite pattern. The events of greatest import have come to me as a gift. I did not get them by aggressively seeking them, no more than I could have predicted being born to fine parents or living in a free country. I accept that my life is in the hands of God, where I find my rest and my destiny.

I am not the kind of person who can find happiness by pushing for it. Every time I try, something goes wrong and I have to start over again. What I want comes to me, not of my own doing. God alone can grant the gift of real happiness. And at a relatively young age, he has given me a taste of the real thing. There is no guarantee I can be faithful. All I can do is fall upon the mercy of my God, who is greater than any of my mistakes.

When I look upon the future, as I often do these days, I find that there is much to be trusted in the pattern of the past: say yes to God and the rest will follow. Live the present moment in the light of the Lord's promise, and all shall be well. Saying yes to what God wants for me involves a risk, but I am sure of this: what God wills is ultimately what makes me or anyone happy. This is my faith; its roots cannot be shaken, whatever else may happen to me.

The mysterious thing is that we often, because of our narrowness of sight, cannot see what things mean until they are behind us. I feel in the depths of my heart that I am on the right track. I am open to whatever God wants of and for me. Should this include husband and children, fine. Should it mean staying single, that is fine, too. I am in the best place to meet a person with whom I would want to share some of the deep commitments described above and to meet the friends who will support me in or outside of marriage.

I guess what I am saying is this: my life is really becoming simple, so I have to be careful not to make it too complex! It consists of saying yes — to life, to the author of all life, to the place that is to be mine in the mystery of providence. And whenever a wave of confidence of this sort overtakes us, you may notice that it leaves in its wake a desire not to say too much about it or to explain it away. For what it's worth, I've never felt more at peace. This kind of certitude leaves plenty of room for occasional doubts, bad moods, and even bouts of the blues. I trust you will understand and accept all sides of me, even those I cannot yet foresee.

Believe me, I do not want this letter to be an apology for my life. What I have done thus far gives me a feeling of satisfaction and inner esteem for myself as a child of God. I must remain open to the things I have yet to do. As I said before, you and Mother are an intimate part of who I am and shall be. Backed by your selfless generosity, I have been able to find my own place in the world. Someone once wrote that it is only in absence that we know what another human being's presence means to us.

Here, amidst the quiet I so cherish, in this, my first apartment, I can come to a new level of appreciation for my upbringing and growth into womanhood, I thank you for making this decision not to live under your roof anymore a separation more pleasant than poignant. You have sought my well-being; now, in this hour of decision, you wish me every blessing.

Please understand that my living away from home has been a way to experience the joy that comes from little things like decorating rooms to my taste, trying out new recipes on willing friends, having a place of privacy where I can reflect in peace.

You know my feelings about solitude and togetherness. I need not repeat them here. I can only assure you of my contentment in the light of the milestone I have recently reached. Let us see what the upcoming years will bring. God willing, they will include good health and a chance to do something to return to others what I have received. Let us enjoy as often as we can a meal together, lots of hugs and kisses, holidays and vacations, quiet times and even a few honest battles! For the rest, let's remember to thank God for what we have been given. Pray that I may find a way to be an embodiment of

God's love, to take the road mapped out by mercy without fear or deviation — for this is the path I must pursue.

With love, Susan

A few days after receiving this letter, Mother wrote to me "for the record":

Dearest Daughter:

Dad and I have read your wonderful letter over and over again. Thank you for taking the time to write it. Dad asked me to read it to him aloud and slowly, and I did. The "old pot of water dropped from his head" and the tears started to flow. He went to bed with this remark: "I thank God Susan knows what is good for her. I pray that God will help her to find it." The next morning he got up and said to me: "Could you get me a cup of coffee and read Susan's letter again, real slow?" Please don't throw it away when we die.

Love, Mom

*A soul rises up, restless with tremen-
dous desire for God's honor and the
salvation of souls. She has for some
time exercised herself in virtue and
has become accustomed to dwelling
in the cell of self-knowledge in
order to know better God's goodness
toward her since upon knowledge
follows love.*

— *Catherine of Siena*

4 ಟಿ

Womanspirit in Search of Self-knowledge

*W*OMEN WHO WANT TO UNDERSTAND the spirit behind the title of this book must be willing to dig deeply into the caverns of memory, imagination, and anticipation that affect all that we are and do. Being candid about the quest for self-knowledge is a challenge, whether one is single or married, childless or a mother, widowed, divorced, separated, or remarried, a lay person in the world or a member of a religious congregation. Women seek to disclose the meaning of life's unfolding, whether they are rich or poor, believers or nonbelievers, young, middle-aged, or elderly. Inquiry of this sort leads frequently to faith sharing. Our sense of church is inseparable from our personal relationship to a personal God. Friends, family, members, co-workers, occasional strangers become directing influences, as I can testify from experience.

I continued my teaching and administrative work at the Institute of Formative Spirituality for over twenty years. Then, in 1988, after a long period of appraisal, I accepted the call to resign my university position and move into full-time ministry in the field of lay formation. I became executive director of the Epiphany Association, a nonprofit ecumenical center devoted to research, publication, and resource development in this field. I had cofounded this organization a few years earlier with Father Adrian van Kaam. We strove with the help of many other people to meet a growing need for adult Christian formation in the modern world, in family life, and in the market place. I identified with women and men who were being drawn to reflect on such questions as "how do I combine professional excellence with whatever God is calling me to be as a spiritual person?" I shared their convictions that we cannot compromise Christ-centered values in the interest of conforming to the expectations of a success-oriented, consumer-driven system. I empathized with young people who were raised as Catholics but who felt increasingly alienated from the institutional church.

I believe the road to spiritual formation leads us to reclaim the treasures of our faith tradition, but I also realize that many look outside the church for answers. In fact I hear more questions than there are convincing responses. Women are asking how can we integrate what we believe and how we live at home and in the work place? How can we be all that God calls us to be in an ecclesial and social climate that still tends to diminish our gifts? Why does authority impose constraints rather than ushering in a new era of oneness in Christ Jesus?

Women will no longer tolerate being treated with disrespect. In the light of Christ's call to discipleship, we seek to turn resentment into reconciliation. We believe that when conversion of heart occurs, injustice will cease. Renewal will become a reality. The mystery of God's love will bring life to dead bones.

There are two faces to this quest for self-knowledge: one is solitude, the other is togetherness. Women need time alone to think, to plan, to get in touch with the stirrings of the spirit, to trust the movements of our heart. My sister-in-law, the mother of three children under twelve, says she feels depleted of physical and spiritual energy if she cannot find time away from everyone. Her oasis moment may be no more than a solitary walk in the backyard or an extra long time in the bath tub. A widow I visit says she has tried in vain to explain to her own and her deceased husband's friends that she honestly does not mind living alone. She enjoys reading, watching television, working on her arts and crafts, cooking, and occasionally entertaining. To me she has confessed a special joy when the door closes on the last guest and once more she can be surrounded by silence.

I trust these self-disclosures. I admire women who break through boundaries in search of our story. I am especially awed when this search leads us in a new way to God and through God to others. Educated by church and society to conform, to please, to put our own needs and desires last on the list, women are finding that self-knowledge enables us to keep the "love others" part of the Great Commandment in dialogue with the part that says "as you love yourself."

Over the years, through correspondence and animated conversation, one friend and I have learned what a life of solitude and togetherness really means. A bonding occurs between women of like spirit that is difficult to describe. We know the feeling in general when we have a friend, male or female, with whom we can pick up a conversation held long ago without missing a beat. This kind of relationship is rare. It enables two people to read between the lines, wait through long pauses while silence facilitates an exchange beyond words, laugh until our bellies ache, and cry together without shame.

My friend once took time from her busy ranch and family life in California to "retreat to a still point." For years we two have shared our love and enthusiasm for the poet T. S. Eliot. We have read aloud and exchanged notes on his *Four Quartets*. One of its lines, "At the still point of the turning world . . . there the dance is . . . ," is special for us because we have both experienced something of this dance that is still and yet moving.

Eliot found the proper paradox to describe what women know to be true from experience. The pain of childbirth becomes pleasure when a healthy baby is born. The thanklessness of routine tasks can be transformed by an unexpected bouquet. The sting of anger over little things may mark the start of a new depth of relationship. The dance of life is both still and moving like the swirl of a ballerina set to defy gravity as her body bounds upward in lightsome grace. Every end constitutes a new beginning like the wrinkled winter bulb tamped underground that blooms lustrous in spring.

The experience of aloneness often accompanies a woman's search for self amidst the thousand demands that fill a day. Getting away from it all is not a luxury for high-spirited types but a survival measure for woman's sanity and spirituality in this fast-paced world. The circumstances of the quest will differ, depending on where we live, on our age and state of health, but the common theme of stepping aside for the sake of starting again is the same. As my friend put it:

What are the lessons of a quest? Is it that we value only what we earn? Is life an ego acquisition of things and experiences that gives us the illusion that we are in control of our destinies? Or does it capture the spirit of humankind in search of completion, longing for the life-giving water that will make us whole? I think it is all of these things and especially the latter. . . .

I thought of the intense sweetness and suffering we have experienced within our family. I felt deeply reconciled to my frequent failure at being my true self, to my frenzy to gain merit and accomplish something, but mostly to the beauty of my life. I wept at the glory of it all and remembered Eliot's lines perhaps not exactly but close enough about the still point amid the dancing — "where past and future are gathered. Neither movement from, nor towards, neither ascent nor decline. Except for the point the still point, there would be no dance, and there is only the dance. . . . The release from action and suffering, release from the inner and the outer compulsion, yet surrounded by a grace of sense, a white light still and moving."

At the end of her retreat, having purposefully fasted, having kept sense stimulation to a minimum, my friend concluded:

Though I knew that there had been no significant transformation, I felt that the peace of these days would affect my life. They would give me the courage to pull away a little more frequently from the tides of my worldly needs. They would beckon me back to being the creature God calls me to be. They would help me not to be deceived by my own deceits, nor appalled by my flaws, nor in despair over the disintegration of our world. But rather, they remind me to live in immense gratitude that I am here, now, as a part of an era that is unleashing the spirit of man/woman in dimensions never before known on this beautiful planet. We have nowhere left to go but inward into ourselves, and from there to our source, upward to God and outward to others.

During and after alone times, women are more able to cope with the ups and downs of daily life, the perks and pains, the aggravations and gains. Things have a way of falling into perspective.

Priorities can be appraised and reset. Solitude becomes a condition for the possibility of remaining open to one's inner self while taking into account the needs and feelings of others. Adds one woman:

> When I walk alone I am not just waiting for company or for a companion. I welcome this space to be at one with myself and my God. I can sometimes savor solitude as a fine wine, sip its cool liquid flow from oneness to allness. No matter how many times I am together with others, I still like to take time to walk alone. This experience is different from being independent. I am dependent on air and water, on food and shelter, on God. But I need space in which to just be me. I need room to breathe free air, to feel life at the marrow.

When solitude gives way, as it does, to service or some sort of active involvement, women are ready to go the full distance. Social service, political action, new and traditional careers, homemaking, child care — the arenas where women act are becoming more diverse by the minute. Women are at ease being volunteers and paid workers. We are not content to sit and wait in the wings anymore. Women are notably proactive, empowered, on the move, targeting oppressive structures and their causes, mandating moral, social, and political change. We seek to go out of ourselves, to minister to others, to use our gifts fully, even if this means having to walk alone. To stand for counter-cultural beliefs is more important to us than to attain cheap and passing popularity.

Alongside these times of aloneness, women admit that the desire to find understanding friends, male and female, runs deep. To belong to some kind of support group, either within a local church community or through an established association, is high on the wish list of most women. Family ties are treasured but so, too, are friendships that give women a chance to share falling-apart and coming-together moments. The need for friendship beyond family affiliations is felt acutely by women who work outside the home, live far away from parents and "old pals," or find that marriage is not in the offing immediately or perhaps never. A friend of mine called to tell me:

> I came to this town three months ago wanting to find a parish that was a community, not just a place where people came to Mass on Sundays. I have been visiting churches in the

area and asking new acquaintances about which churches are active and involved in community building. I find as usual that a lot depends on the openness or closure of the pastor. I'm resigned to engaging in this inquiry for a while longer.

The women who responded to my questionnaire were not inclined to sit at home feeling sorry for themselves. On the contrary, all were desirous of helping other people, of expressing hospitality and acting decisively, with compassion, in the face of suffering. A sense of ministry has overtaken Catholic women, especially since Vatican Council II with its emphasis on social presence. Women want to reach out and help others in need. We are ready to respond. Where this call will lead is not readily clear, but its expression has to be rooted in faith lest the energy needed to see a task through to the end erode or disappear entirely. Unless our sense of service is inspired by a transcendent vision, the demands of work become overwhelming.

Among women religious, it ought to come as no surprise how absorbing a ministerial sense can be and how it can cast a shade of ambiguity on one's sense of self-identity. "We are more than the work we do, but we have worked for so long under the weight of apostolic worth only that it is not easy to value as highly who we are." New forms of ministry are as much in the process of evolving as are new ways of seeking personal and spiritual enrichment. "Nuns," as a sister friend said to me, "will never again be seen as finished products rolling off assembly lines." She added: "Our lives evidence as much confusion and ambiguity as we find in the general population. All of us are in the transition, the church included."

All of us, in other words, are on the way to self-emergence and the disclosure of new forms of church and community life. It is often easier to tell people what we do as professionals than it is to put our finger on who we are uniquely called to be. Projects paid and volunteered for are occasions to expend energy, be creative, function well. But that is not enough to fill the empty space many women feel inside. This space beckons us not to become fixated on any thing that stops short of the goal of intimacy with God, or as one person said, "the lived experience of a deeper mystery."

> I am always searching for something to give meaning to life underneath all my accomplishments and failures, something

that endures, that forms a resource in which I can re-source myself.

Using our gifts and talents as a means to embody who we most deeply are is the secret of any successful ministry. I found out how important the connection between being and doing was when I returned from my post-collegiate tour of Europe. I was not only slightly depressed, since to depart from a person or place one loves is to die a little; I was also unemployed. The positions that had been open immediately after graduation were filled over the summer. It was not easy for a woman in my city to find work in journalism under any circumstances and now it was impossible. I pounded the pavements until early December, then decided to forego pride and take a position as a sales clerk in a downtown department store, ostensibly to add to my repertoire of book knowledge some real experience in retail advertising.

Fortunately for me one of my old bosses went shopping shortly before Christmas. He spotted me behind the sweater counter where he was looking for a gift for his girlfriend. Surprised to see me there, he asked what my plans were. I said I still hoped to find work in the field of public relations. As luck would have it, he was in a top position with the United Jewish Federation and promptly asked if I would like to be his assistant. I resigned from retailing the next day and was, before year's end, working happily with the Jewish community to ready promotion for the upcoming campaign. I knew when I started the job that the work was only temporary but six months later — just when I thought I would have to start going through the help-wanted ads again — I was asked to join the staff of the prestigious *Jewish Chronicle* as a society editor.

While these changes were occurring, I had enrolled in night school at the University of Pittsburgh with the intention of pursuing a master's degree in English literature. Though at the time I could only manage one course a semester, I loved the study. I had begun to realize that a part of me would remain unfulfilled without it. As a matter of fact, the more I dared to listen to the voices within, the more I had to admit that something was wrong with my life direction. I had tried to convince myself that a career in journalism was what I wanted. Now I had an enviable position, one that could lead me to New York or Chicago where the action was. But the more I tried to find the link between what I was doing and who I was, the greater the chasm, the deeper the confusion.

I can remember as if it were yesterday a moment of sheer ego desperation. I was attending an important festivity to gather information for a story. It was October 1966. Dessert was being served. I tried to make small talk with my table companions. Suddenly I found myself gagging on the words. I literally could not speak. I pretended to be choking and asked to be excused. I did not go to the women's room. Instead I fled as fast as my legs would carry me to the nearest exit and went out into the crisp fall night gasping for air. I was afraid I would faint. That's when I looked up at the stars and knew it was time to pray my peasant prayer — the prayer of absolute faith-filled abandonment that God will show the way. I had to know what I was supposed to do with my life. I could not believe that at a time when by outside standards I had achieved my heart's desire, I never felt unhappier. What was wrong? Where was the divine plan for my life now? I needed help, and there was no way I could give it to myself.

Luckily, there was no one on the street because I said all of this aloud. Drained as I was by this outburst of emotion and longing, I felt strangely at peace. I went back to dinner as if nothing had happened and thought no more of the incident until several weeks later when I received a call from the chairman of the communications department at Duquesne University telling me that Father Adrian van Kaam would like to see me for reasons he would explain when I arrived for a scheduled interview. Convinced that the encounter had something to do with publicity for the institute he had founded in 1963, I had no idea that this meeting would change my life and set me at last on the path of integrating who I was with what God was calling me to do. Though I left the editorial field in the formal sense to become the first assistant director of the institute, I brought with me to this position the training I had gathered administratively as well as my skills as a writer. All would be put to good use in this new form of service. I began to sense what lay ministry might entail and how I might become a creative participant in the emerging field of formative spirituality.

Women have always contributed to traditional fields like education and health care at home and in the community at large. Now, for the first time, we are being drawn into decision-making positions that will change church and society forever. I was on the ground floor of one innovative movement, but I was among many women who would be able to look back over a relatively short span of time and cite quantum leaps in the level of our participation in all walks of life. Affirmative action was beginning to have good effects in guaranteeing women equal pay for equal work, though in some circles the "leaps" were more like "baby steps."

Almost from the start I felt a sense of purpose. I could see progress in my ministry where before I had to cope with a pervasive fear of stagnation. I watched with delight as certain stereotypes crumbled, such as equating knowledge of Christian spirituality strictly with formation in a religious community. As a lay person, I must admit to feeling at times like a fish out of water, but so be it. The future would tell its own tale. There was no use being fixated on the past. What mattered was being present here and now. I simply trusted that the Spirit to whom Pope John XXIII had opened wide the windows of the church would guide us where we were meant to go.

"Look at what has to be done and laugh," was a lesson I learned early in life from my mother and my grandmother. Laughter never fails to rekindle waning energy. It reminds me that our best laid plans invariably go astray. While we cannot always detect God's wink in the middle of the show, we can be sure there is more going on than meets the eye. "It's next to impossible," Mother would say, "to put a good woman down." When she was five years old, crouching under the kitchen table because she had "rickets" and could not walk without tripping, neighbors would breeze in and ask my grandmother, who had lost several children to one disease or another, "Isn't the little rat dead yet?," not realizing or caring that Mother was under the table absorbing everything they said. She often told me: "I decided then and there to fool them."

Women have been "fooling" people for a long time. We are dubbed the "weaker sex," but statistics prove we live longer than most men. Women like Mary are natural-born magicians, able to transform preposterous situations like the one at Cana ("they have no wine for the wedding party") into happy endings ("most hosts serve the choice wine first but you have saved the best for last"). History is richer because of the work of "magicians" like Catherine of Genoa, Joan of Arc, Jeanne de Chantal, Katherine Drexel, and Dorothy Day.

I believe magic is being released every day from contemplative centers where our sisters pray for peace; in orphanages where children find a home; in houses of the dying where limbs are washed and readied for a dignified burial; in soup kitchens where the homeless are clothed and fed; in migrant camps where homes are held together in tents and trailers by feminine tenacity and expressions of tenderness that put to shame "macho" show-offs; in centers where unwed mothers are learning respect for life and choosing adoption over abortion; in churches where religious education programs would collapse were women not willing to sacrifice time and energy to teach God's word. The magic flows every day from slums to schools, from single-parent homes to nuclear families, from farms to factories, from pro-life rallies and marches for peace to people power in Eastern bloc countries. Women are there, side by side with men, to work a little magic.

Rather than rest in an achieved position of leadership, one sister I know, a member of the National Black Sisters Conference, set as her goal to "within one year...be known in the community" in the South where she is assigned and "to have at least one active program going" to do budget counseling for low-income people. This is the kind of magic I mean. It reminds me of a proverb from the Christopher ministry I often repeat: "It is better to light one candle than to curse the darkness."

Women are igniting thousands of tapers in our time. We see their faces on television as they walk for freedom in South Africa; seek their arrested and tortured children in South and Central America; unite to press charges to the full extent of the law against rapists, drunk drivers, abortionists, pornographers, pimps, drug pushers, and every destructive element in society. On these front lines women of all faith groupings join together to mandate social justice. Catholic women support the bishops in their call in pastoral documents for an end to nuclear war and its excessive weaponry and their insistence on the just distribution of economic goods.

Women benefit from cultivating a historical perspective on life. We need to remember the past if we are to renew the present and pave the way for our daughters and sons to have a happier future. As one astute observer said:

> This perspective gives texture and solidity to my life. I see myself as part of, not central to, the whole fabric of civilization.

While I know I am unique, at the same time, I am so much a piece of the whole that this belonging is at once a marvel, disrupting complacency, and a comfort, evoking peace.

Women see history not as a static list of facts but as a dynamic story. They rename history as also "her story." God, for instance, has been depicted over the ages as an impatient, stern, punishing patriarch. Women are resurrecting another image — that of God as mercy, as a nurturing mother, a God of love who welcomes all in quest of goodness, truth, and beauty, a Holy Other who educates by encounters with the harshness of reality but who does not cripple self-initiative nor destroy the desire for justice.

Creative hands can make a difference. A discerning eye can behold beauty and harmony where the less discerning see only scars and chaos. Who of us has not gone into a hotel or a retreat house and, after a lightning-speed appraisal, changed a pillow here, added a flower to a vase there, or placed a piece of furniture where it really belongs. These small gestures signify a woman's need to make a mosaic of meaning out of an otherwise mundane moment. Not only do such touches embody our aesthetic bent; they reveal our need to personalize a place rather than to let it remain nondescript, our capacity to see in the ordinary a pointer to a higher mystery. Annie Dillard in her book of expeditions and encounters entitled *Teaching a Stone to Talk* puts it this way:

> You know what it is to open up a cottage. You barge in with your box of groceries and your duffelbag full of books. You drop them on a counter and rush to the far window to look out. I would say that coming into a cottage is like being born, except we do not come in to the world with a box of groceries and a duffelbag full of books — unless you want to take these as metonymic symbols for culture. Opening up a summer cottage is like being born in this way: at the moment you enter, you have all the time you are ever going to have.

This commitment to preserve original beauty is not without tension. As another seeker said:

> I am ever in danger of going out to solve the great problems of the world rather than staying in to manage the ones placed at my own feet. I am committed to God on the vertical bar of the cross and hence to God's people on the horizontal.

To make history "her story" requires hard, honest effort, commingled with patience when things do not go as we planned or happen overnight. For every disclosure there is another chapter to divulge. At the same time we know and we do not know where the Spirit is leading us in these changing times. I used to wonder if I passed myself on the street, would I recognize who I was. What do I really look like in God's eyes? Do I care too much about how I appear in the eyes of other people? Can I honestly appreciate what I behold each day in the mirror?

Under scrutiny of this sort, confidence wanes. I tend to see what is wrong more than what is right. A woman I counseled wondered if she would ever be loved or appreciated enough. She never really felt wanted by her parents. To be self-affirming is for her a continual struggle. Yet she refuses to give up. The enemy, she now realizes, is not God or her family or the world but her own self-perception. As a survivor, she knows this image of her womanhood can change. Her inner beauty will never disappear. No outside force can destroy it.

To be a survivor can breed anger or resentment. It can harden one's heart and carve harsh lines around one's lips. But suffering can have the opposite effect. It can evoke in a noble heart feelings of empathy; lips can soften with tender sighs of compassion for vulnerable others — for relatives trapped in tense marriages, for victims of terminal disease, for children with learning disabilities. The list of broken ones is endless. They need a woman's touch to mediate God's mercy, to anchor them in God's love, even while their ship is pulling away from port.

Women know what it is like to weep and pray that life will be otherwise while knowing that there is no why for innocent suffering. A woman's child dies of a rare disease. She cradles the little one in her arms. "Your baby is dead," the neighbors tell her. "But she is still warm," the mother says. She rocks the child softly as if she were asleep. While the body is warm, she will not let go.

Some days in the lives of women are worse than others. Many are as sad as this story. A child departs this world, but a mother has to decide to go on living. Her wings have been clipped, but she has the power to soar free — she has her womanspirit:

> I seen a lotta life and death. Now I know my time is comin',
> but I get to choose when it's gonna be. Sometimes I wake
> in my bed in the mornin' and I say to myself, "How about

today? How about if you just don't get up?" And I lie there for a while and then reach for my pills and I know it ain't gonna be today. You know, I still got some books left to read.

— Another passage from *The Quilters*

5

*And because I am a woman in-
volved in practical cares, I cannot
give the first half of the day to these
things, but must meditate when I
can, early in the morning and on
the fly during the day. Not in the
privacy of a study — but here, there
and everywhere — at the kitchen table, on the train, on the ferry, on my
way to and from appointments and
even while making supper or putting
Teresa [her daughter] to bed.*
— Dorothy Day

Womanspirit in Touch
with the World

*B*EHIND EVERY "I am" statement women make in the search for
self-knowledge there is a whole person in a situation — a woman
formed and deformed by relationships, a woman responsible for
others while striving to find her own place in the world.

Marriage and children remain for many women the first priority. Commitments made to those who depend on her deepen
with age. Aging means fewer choices but more contentment with
what is. "It is wonderful just to be, without pretense." This mother
and grandmother admits in hindsight that she was immature when
she got married. She was full of expectations, but had none of the
wisdom necessary to make her marriage work. "The church tries
to prepare couples more now than it did then." I asked her why
she stayed married. "Not because things were always good, but
because I believed in the sacrament of matrimony, in marriage as
instituted by God...in family life as the basic unit of society."
Having made a vow for life, she knew it would be within her marriage that she had to work out her salvation. For her it would have
been inconceivable to enter married life, as many do today, "with
a divorce mentality."

Child raising gave me an abiding sense of what is worthwhile despite all the work — and motherhood is hard. It is physically and emotionally draining, with or without day care centers. But there are many moments when parenting is satisfying, creative, fulfilling to spouses, and fun. Looking back over all the mistakes we made, the crises, the trauma, I would still do it again. My daughter has a more difficult life than I because she is a single parent. She says having me as a grandmother is a grace, but frankly I can only do so much. I try to help her see that God does give us the grace to cope with what comes.

I believe that trust in grace is the one outcome of a Catholic upbringing women do not take for granted. At age fifty-four, the mother of a large family says she relied on grace to help her foster over twenty newborns until they could be adopted or returned to their parents. She credits faith in God's grace as the source of her strength. "There were moments when I reached low points, but I always knew where my roots were. Grace was the wellspring from which I could always draw cool water." The fruits of commitment outweighed the suffering she had to undergo with bureaucratic red tape, personal fatigue, and fear that the children she loved would not receive the attention they deserved. "If I tried to take all of this on my shoulders without turning the end results over to God . . . I would never have taken on this volunteer project nor sought a second career in nursing."

Maybe the old saying that God writes straight with crooked lines is the best definition of grace we can find. This is the legacy of solid Catholic formation in family and school life. Younger women are often the first to admit that they sometimes find themselves floundering morally and spiritually because they lack a similar solid foundation.

If there is one theme that recurs when womanspirit is in touch with the real world, it is this: "Count your blessings, things could always be worse." A single teacher in the autumn of her life remembers her many pupils and experiences God's love extending through her to them. A retired bank teller credits her husband of forty-two years as being her greatest treasure because "he was beside me all through my crazy juggling of family and church activities, never discouraging me from flapping my wings even if it meant he had to cook dinner for the children." A waitress beyond retirement believes aging is nothing to worry about "as long as you keep active, make other people happy, pray daily, and never indulge in self-pity. . . . I even tell some of my customers that Jesus' gifts of peace and joy are the best cure for depression."

I could not help but wonder if women the world over were quilters would they end up choosing the same colors to form common patterns: blue for sad times, green for days of hope, yellow for sunny dispositions, purple for dark nights, white for God's grace, red for eternal life. Just as quilters stitch many shades and shapes into one cover, so women combine many feelings and experiences into one life of love and service. Reform in church and society may be slow in coming, but womanspirit is never stagnant, never averse to accepting new challenges, never indifferent to those in need. Womanspirit exists in time but its capacity to be in touch with God's way for the world is eternal. Women give and go on giving, even when the returns are minimal and honors are not forthcoming. It is agreed that dwelling on the past is as futile as fretting about the unknown future. All one has is the present moment. The place of grace's mysterious guidance is here; the blessings we need are given now.

> I suffered a nervous breakdown several years ago and my mother would not, because she said she could not, come to see me. Even when I recovered, she would steel herself for a visit from me and did not encourage them. She had had a breakdown herself and could not bear my intensity lest she lose control again. . . . But I love her and will go on loving her because God has given me the grace here and now to rise from the hell of a shattered selfhood and make of me an epiphany of love divine.

As a caregiver herself, this woman has found healing in her ministry to others who suffer from depression and a desire to close themselves off from a cruel world. She has found that coldness is only the mask people who need to draw close wear to insulate themselves from hurt. "I could have spent years soothing my fragile ego, but instead I responded to the invitation of grace to enfold suffering in my arms wherever I see it." If such love brings tears to our eyes, it is because we realize that magnanimity of heart is a rare gift. Paradoxically God gives it to those who feel least worthy of it. This woman admits that she is no paragon of virtue; she is as weak and wounded as anyone. She would never qualify as a legendary lover of the less fortunate. "I am," she says, "only an ordinary woman who makes beds, cooks meals, feels taken for granted, gets angry, but I have learned to pray my way through all of these experiences and to let God use me as he will." Her prayer is this:

> Lord, Jesus, give them what they need, those gathered under my roof and those far away, the homeless and tempest-tossed, give them the love that alone heals and bestows life — that same astounding love that has set me free.

Womanspirit at its finest is like an open door to a warm room on a cold night. All who cross the threshold know that they shall meet a hostess capable of offering them the gift of unconditional love. By contrast, womanspirit at its worst is only able to offer what I call "string love." That is to say: the "I'll love you if you stop being so intense" string or the "I'll hold you if you do what I tell you" string or the "Keep me safe but don't expect me to return the favor" string. Love that wears a selfish face can become a collection of strings, a massive effort at manipulation. It takes the sheer grace of God to help us rise above the temptation to self-centeredness and become truly self-giving. Seduction can pose as compassion. We can treat others as mirrors of our big-heartedness, as consolation prizes awarded to us for gestures of good will. Controlling mothers can seduce children to do what they want by arousing excessive guilt feelings. Lovers can manipulate each other's feelings for pleasure's sake or mere self-gratification. "I love you" can become the three emptiest words in the English language if love is not combined with commitment and the intention to support unconditionally another's well-being.

Love that is true is not the greeting card variety but the human, thereby always limited, equivalent of God's own unconditional outreach to us personally and as a people. If God needed to *feel* love to *give* love, would God's only begotten ever have consented to being nailed on a cross? Out of the dust of cruelest suffering came our salvation. The training course for committed love is often an occasion that causes a woman to suffer. When this woman needed her mother the most, her mother did not welcome her visit. Such pain can shrivel a heart or render it more tender. The choice is ours: to stay in the ashes of resentment or watch the phoenix of forgiveness soar free.

When Thérèse of Lisieux was trying to discern her vocation, she thought perhaps she was called to be a missionary in China, but the next cough told her that she had to stay in the convent. A nun with tuberculosis could not travel. There had to be another answer. The saint saw that her vocation was to love God and others wholly in the place where she was. On earth as in heaven she could scatter the roses of love and let their sweet scent spread from Carmel to the farthest corners of the cosmos. Thérèse allowed God, her Divine Lover, to take her in her utter humanness and transform her into fire. She records this intense moment of recognition in her autobiography, *The Story of a Soul*:

> *Charity* gave me the key to my *vocation*. I understood that if the Church had a body composed of different members, the most necessary and most noble of all could not be lacking to it, and so I understood that the Church *had a Heart and that this Heart* was BURNING WITH LOVE. *I understood it was Love alone* that made the Church's members act, that if *Love* ever became extinct, apostles would not preach the Gospel and martyrs would not shed their blood. I understood that LOVE COMPRISED ALL VOCATIONS, THAT LOVE WAS EVERY THING, THAT IT EMBRACED ALL TIMES AND PLACES.... IN A WORD, THAT IT WAS ETERNAL!
>
> Then, in the excess of my delirious joy, I cried out: O Jesus, my Love ... my *vocation*, at last I have found it ... MY VOCATION IS LOVE!
>
> Yes, I have found my place in the Church and it is You, O my God, who have given me this place; in the heart of the Church, my Mother, I shall be *Love*. Thus I shall be everything, and thus my dream will be realized.

Women who are creative think differently from others. They are amazed to find that they do not see the world the way others do.

> For example, I rarely show up at an occasion dressed in the manner of the crowd. I am certain that I will be and yet I rarely am. Once my husband and I were invited to a bicentennial party, and we were to dress historically as someone from America's past. I went dressed as Abraham

Lincoln, whom I admire, and he went as my freed, black slave woman. Everyone — EVERYONE — of the other 148 people were dressed as Dolly Madison and George Washington complete in knee-britches, white stockings, powdered wigs and crinoline dresses. . . . I'm also a good cook, but I never follow the recipes in the book. Is this rebellion or creativity? I can read a recipe and decide how to alter it and am, to my taste, rarely wrong, with one minor hitch: my children don't like my cooking and long for what they call "American" food: hot dogs, pizza, hamburgers, and fried chicken!

This humorous original is full of spunk and fortitude. She is disinclined to conform to the crowd. She enjoys her culinary concoctions, even if no one else does. Her experience reminds me of an event that occurred once a year when I was a child, the annual preparation and serving of tripe stew. For a long time, neither I nor my brothers knew what the tidbits we were chewing actually were. They did not taste too bad, especially since they were coated in the garlicky, fresh tomato and basil sauce we loved. But the minute we learned the origin of tripe, its being the lining of a cow's stomach, we delegated Mom and Dad to devour this delicacy alone. All we wanted was good old "American" food.

The creativity displayed at the costume party points to the truth that women of spirit resist conformity to crowds. The crowd is faceless. It seeks to level originality and treats with contempt anyone who is different. I have been the brunt of the levelling mentality many times in my life. I know from experience how much it can hurt. Instead of recognizing and respecting each other's gifts and talents, we women can make one another the object of envy and jealousy. When I was a senior in college, studying journalism, I entered a writing contest sponsored by one of our city papers. Much to my amazement, my entry won first place. The dinner honoring the winners was held at an elegant press club. Since I was the main awardee, I was the third in line to approach the podium for my plaque. By the time my turn came, my hands were shaking and my throat was dry because I had to make a short acceptance speech. Once I began, I relaxed and all went well. When it was over, I felt on top of the world, but couldn't wait to get to the powder room! A few girls from my class came in after me. Not realizing I was there, they proceeded to rip my words apart, suggesting that because I was editor of the school paper I had been treated with favoritism. For all they knew, I may have "brown-nosed" the judges. That was the last straw. I had intended to hide in the stall until they left, but could not resist the chance to confront them, not with words but with stony silence. Holding back my tears, I left the cubicle and stood for a moment behind them as they were primping in front of the mirror. I muttered something like "You've made my day," and moved out. We stayed clear of one another for weeks thereafter, too embarrassed to speak. Soon enough it was time for graduation. Our group drifted to the four winds, but the ache of that experience has never quite gone away. Later, in a more forgiving mood, I tried to talk to God: "What can you expect of us? We are sheep. We are so foolish that we would choose our own way over Yours. If nothing else proves our folly, surely this must. How can we be otherwise? You made us. You know us. We are dust. Do not expect from us that which is not within us. It is foolishness on my part — this self-will, yet I was hurt. Help me to forgive and forget."

Conversing with God in unabashed candor is never easy. Praying does not depend on mental gymnastics or lofty theological abstractions. It is more like banter or inner argumentation or story telling. As long as it is real, as long as we hide nothing from God of what we are really feeling — anger and joy, frustration and thanksgiving — our prayer is good. Would God who made us little words in the Divine Word expect more from us than this kind of word-play? God sees the innocent child in us and our rebellious pride. God hears our pleas for forgiveness and our cravings for revenge. God accepts our worry words and our surrender, our selfish motives and our selfless moments. Like sailors marooned in a leaky boat on tumultuous seas, so we await rescue by a loving God. We long to grasp the lifeline between us and our Creator. When God comes, we are as excited as Peter, who leapt out of the boat and into the water to walk to Jesus, freed from the force of gravity by his faith. As long as his heart remained buoyant with transcendent hope, the big fisherman did not sink. Then his mind, with its doubts and reasoning, took charge, clipping the wings of his abandoned flight, and Peter cried like a baby, "Lord, save me, I'm lost!"

Jesus saw behind the façade of rebellion, loneliness, and injured pride the original image and likeness to God in which all are created. Like a mother looks upon children who are naughty with tenderness, so Jesus regarded women and men with respect. He

never viewed women as chattel, as did the men of his Middle Eastern tradition. Once when a woman was about to be stoned to death
for adultery, he silenced the murderous crowd and offered her a
second chance. He evoked by his love the self-initiative that led to
her reforming an otherwise lost life. Like a sculptor, Jesus chipped
away at the prostituted veneer of Magdalene and found a faithful messenger. Underneath the bravado of Peter, he discovered a
veritable rock on which to build his church.

These miracles of transformation happen every day. A mother
takes in stride her teenager's outburst of anger and serves her a cup
of tea. A nurse looks beyond a needle-pocked arm to a sick spirit
that needs a hug more than a sleeping pill. A teacher refuses to
believe that a slow learner is on the borderline of retardation and
finds out that dyslexia is the problem. In myriad ways, the image of
God is disclosed by people who are foolish enough to love without
affixing any price to their self-gift. Every day someone on earth
sees the face of God in a suffering person. Every day in earthen
vessels treasure untold is revealed. For me, this kind of miracle
happened in, of all places, a K-Mart.

When I moved into my own home in 1985, my goal, besides
supervising its construction, was to become more efficient in small
repairs. A toilet that would not stop running put to the test my
do-it-yourself intention. Following a quick conversation with my
brother to ascertain the item I needed to complete work on the
commode, I headed for K-Mart, a well-stocked self-help store, an-
ticipating no problem. My brother had told me the aisle where
the gadget could be procured. Overcoming my general dislike for
hands-on places packed with merchandise and few salespersons, I
resolved to find what I needed with a minimum of searching. After
twenty minutes, I admitted defeat and slumped over to the cus-
tomer service phone. Another twenty-minute wait ensued when
at last a woman, perhaps forty years old, stormed down the aisle,
with an air of resentment as if I were to blame for her bad day. In
a disgusted, accusatory tone of voice, she said, "Hey, Lady, what's
your problem?"

Everything in me wanted nothing more at that moment than to
tell her off. It was not I but she and this whole stupid system that
was at fault. She was not a person to me but merely an extension
of an impersonal production line. Quickly my mind formulated a
cutting remark. I was about to deliver it when grace intervened

and restrained my tongue. I saw myself at a crossroads. I could de-personalize another human being or turn the tables in favor of her dignity. Amazingly, not I, but Christ in me, responded to her slur with a heartfelt look of compassion and the words, "You must be having a miserable day." She was taken aback and then blurted out, "How did you know?" In a lightning flash, there in the hardware section, "Irene" and I had an experience of genuine togetherness. It turned out that she was a single parent with two young children at home under her mother's care. She had been on the floor since opening time without a break because it was a summer Sunday and the store was short of personnel. She was needed at home, but her relief was late. Now she had to deal with my plumbing prob-lem. At that we both laughed. I said I could come back tomorrow evening, but, no, she would go into the stockroom and bring out what was missing from the shelf. No wonder I could not find it. I offered to accompany her so we could talk some more. Would that be okay? Well, it was against the rules . . . but no supervisors were around . . . so why not? Since I was a teacher, could she ask me something about her little girl's learning problem. . . .

When we chip away at the worst in us, we still find the "im-mortal diamond" that is the "image of God." Irene helped me to see that faith in this image is not foolishness but the fulcrum of divine wisdom. I was ready to explode at one of the *anawim*, had not grace stemmed the vitriolic tide. The inconvenience I had come to the store to resolve was nothing compared to her suffering. The mystery of God's love conveyed a message not to be forgotten through an unlikely medium. Irene taught me again what it means to carry the cross and keep on walking, to flow with rather than against the rhythms of each day. In that rhythm there is a balance rejuvenating in and of itself. I like to take long walks that provide time for prayer and relaxation, time to re-examine priorities, eval-uate decisions, assess relationships. I enjoy time for creativity, for reflection, for imagining how I can implement what I am learning with how I want to live. Instead of seeing my day as a series of "pieces," it becomes a whole, integrated expression of who I am and want to become: a loving person responsive to the love of God and others.

Can we women ever describe who we are without using words like "rhythm," "flow," "rejuvenation"? Can we tell of ourselves without simultaneously speaking of others, of our relationships with friends, peers, colleagues, family, and community members? Time to walk, pray, converse, relate is never wasted. Like the artist who paints with no concept of time passing and suddenly steps back to behold a completed canvas, so woman's time to be present activates her creative potential, her sense of communion with all that is. We women are fast becoming experts in managing "segments" of reality. Here's my career track, there's an afternoon open to shop and clean, but when will I find time to read, exercise, study, pray? The danger is that we risk losing our gift to see the "whole." Is this danger imminent or is it already here?

> My life is such that most of my time is spent with people. I get along well with people, but am quickly drained if I don't have time alone. . . . I . . . work hard at being present to people in an outgoing manner. I have a sense of responsibility and will stay with a job or project to the end, successful or not. According to other people, I am good at organizing, seeing the situation for what it is, but I become impatient when it takes others longer to get there.

Being "quickly drained," "working hard," "organizing well," "becoming impatient," if experienced in excess, are hardly openings to a holistic spirituality that draws together a woman's body, mind, emotions, and longing for God. The latter expressions sound so mercantile, so lacking in receptivity to the "More Than." Women are becoming workaholics. Many confess that they seldom enjoy the grace of religious experiences because they are too busy — juggling schedules, being parents, often without the help of a spouse, striving to advance their careers, only to discover one dark day that their biological clock has run out or that sexual intimacy cut off from committed marital love is as lonely as a train whistle on the Texas plains.

Catholic women are unhappy when their life loses its center in God and begins to shred in small pieces: a one-night stand may feel good for a moment, but it leaves one feeling more than ever alone; a job that pays fairly but offers no spiritual fulfillment takes its toll in due time. These fragments may be all that is left of a woman's life if we lose our sense of the whole. Is there some way we can regain it?

> The things I enjoy most are solitary occupations: prayer and meditation, reading, gardening, and time alone outdoors.

I have been involved in several volunteer activities in the last few years, including tutoring a child from a low-income inner-city family, visiting the elderly in nursing homes, and befriending a woman with a history of mental illness.

These types of involvement (solitary walks, volunteer work, befriending those in need) are at once healing and rewarding to women. They restore our openness to the whole and holy. The solitude-solidarity connection is a recurrent theme in feminine spirituality. I remember in this regard the summer of 1982, when I wrote my book *Celebrating the Single Life*.

My doctors had warned me a few years earlier that a hysterectomy was in the offing, but I still felt disbelief that the surgery had occurred. Yet here I was lying on a lounge chair in the backyard by Mother's vegetable garden, saved from serious disease but minus the potential to bear children. The sun was beating down on a body that belonged to me but had changed radically. I played a few mental games with these stark facts, but no amount of reflection could alter the medical prognosis: six to eight weeks of recovery physically and God only knew how long a process spiritually.

I knew I had to own my singleness in a more radical way. My parenting would have to be a nurture of a different sort — through teaching, writing, speaking, befriending.... The aloneness I felt had to undergo a transformation. Could I shift from the pain of loneliness to the joy of solitude and solidarity with God and others? Certainly not on the basis of my own will power. I had to rely wholly on God's grace and the mediating love of other people. In the ending of one way of life, I had to find a new beginning.

One way of healing proved spiritually to be the way of identification. I tried through reading and meditation to identify with women everywhere who felt loss and separation, whose plans, once thought to be certain, had fallen to pieces; women who were loved and then left in the cold; immigrant and refugee women who managed family life with few, if any, support systems; spiritual mothers from the early desert tradition, who advised seekers how to find God; saintly women, who initiated new works in the church. All of them experienced the grace of spiritual generativity in one way or another. Would I? Could I?

Each day during the recuperation period I would rise, bathe, and rub my dry skin lovingly and tenderly with fragrant oils. It was important especially to touch the area around the incision. I, of course, allowed Mother to pamper me with tasty breakfasts of homemade toast and honey, then, dressed loosely and coolly, I would sink into my old chair, pen and paper in hand, and begin to write this most experiential book about the spirituality of single persons in the world. Writing was undoubtedly therapeutic. The creative act had about it, and still does, the aura of giving birth. Any woman who has had this particular surgery knows how significant this analogy was to me. The solitude-solidarity theme added to my growing understanding of womanspirit, echoed in a friend's observation about her own singleness:

> Being introspective and reflective, having worked to know myself (my father told me once that I have always had "big shoulders" for others to cry or lean on), has helped me to work better with and for others. . . . I have been told that I have the spiritual gift of mercy (the ability to love those individuals whom others find unlovable) and of encouragement.

I cannot begin to describe how important my close friends were to me that summer. Their hugs made me happy. Their unwavering support was the horizon against which this time of private appraisal slowly gave way to new direction disclosures and decisions. I had to reform my life in a number of ways. This work had to be done alone, but others' confirmation was essential. I began to see meaning in what had hitherto appeared meaningless. The truth of my deliberations had to be tested with those whose judgment I trusted. The gift of friendship became one of the keys to celebrating a single life. The same woman quoted above said of her own experience:

> I had come more and more to enjoy . . . the easy familiarity of old friends. My favorite things are to laugh, to pray, to be with someone else who loves me. My friends encourage me to do many of the "things women don't usually do" like spending one summer traveling around the country in my van, buying an old house in a historic district, supervising much of the restoration work myself. . . .

Human friends are important, but so are the friends we find in nature, in pets. "A long walk in the woods with my dog, a day of quiet fishing," refresh my friend. For me, revitalization inevitably occurs when I spend time with my nephews and niece, meandering around the zoo, licking ice cream cones as if there were no tomorrow, or, in their wise words, just "listening to the grass grow."

Nipping at the edges of joy during that summer of healing and creative writing were the "snapping turtles," as I named them, of anxiety (would I have the courage to live alone in the light of my life call were that my destiny?); of self-pity (am I still in the minds of others, in my own imaging, a whole woman?); of anger (did things *really* have to turn out this way? Couldn't God have been a little more subtle about my singleness?) The "turtle" of depression snapped away, too.

One day I asked a friend to share with me her feelings after her husband died. She compared depression to quicksand. She would wake up toward morning — always a special time for her and her husband — slide her hand to the other side of the bed and reel each time from the same shocking sensation of cold sheets. Then the quicksand would appear. She would see herself walking slowly around the rim of the morass. It was so tempting to step in, to let herself be smothered by sand, sucked down into oblivion. She was also aware that if she put even one foot forward, there was no turning back. Before long, she would be in up to her thighs, then over her breasts, and around her neck — then lost entirely.

As she moved through this scene imaginatively, she would break out in sweat. An immense struggle of emotions and will ensued. She reached the point where reason failed, and she had only one recourse: to run as fast as she could from the quicksand and get on with the business of life.

The quicksand was depression. My friend warned me in her common sense way not to try to deal with it emotionally, but to make a cognitive commitment to run away, to change course, to channel energy into a new purpose, to choose joy, to feel grateful for the good times and let the past go. "You've got to let it go," she said, "There's a part of you that simply isn't there anymore, but look at all that is left — all that still gives life to you and love to so many around you." Hers was sound advice, solid words to absorb in solitude. They helped me through the summer when, frankly, I had to run from the quicksand on more than one occasion.

There was another danger, drawn forth by a friend who had also had severe bouts with anxiety and depression: "I... tended to take on more work than I should, ... being strong, professional, and direct." She struggled to keep the balance between doing and being, and so did I. I knew enough about myself to see that this compensatory plunge into work, work, and more work was starting to happen. Functioning for quite a while became a cover-up for my personal vulnerability. I was afraid to disclose to any but a few of my closest friends how frightened I was. No doubt many others received the opposite impression. I had to pay the price of being misunderstood until I stopped using work as a defense against human weakness and began to admit to myself, to God, and others, that I was after all only human and needed their help.

Pride got in the way of candor and compassion for my own and others' vulnerability. Tempering this pseudo-toughness required several doses of disappointment and many different flavors of failure, but slowly and gradually a shift to a more transcendent posture began to take place. Projects became servant sources of prayerful presence, not the main meaning in my life. What I had to do to keep my promises, I did; but I learned to take more time to "listen to the grass grow," to blend the contemplative and active sides of living, to pay attention to the process of living and not to focus solely on producing an end product. In this time of transition, I was reminded of another woman's plight:

> I tend to be undemonstrative and a hard task-master at home and have inflicted pain upon my family while pushing them "for their own good." I pushed a husband through college and graduate school, a son through college and two other children to revolt. And at what price? My husband has just told me he's leaving me to go into a "slower life," pursuing his hobby, and I am on my own, or will be, in a few months.

Our heart aches for her. Would the outcome have been different if somewhere, before it was too late, someone who cared had told her to slow down, not to push so hard at the risk of sacrificing her womanhood. This same woman is an ardent Catholic, who admits having imbibed the directive that hard work is in itself virtue and that imposing your values on others and slaving for them while you forget entirely about your own needs is a sure road to sanctity.

Having a good will and striving to do what is best for all concerned is a noble trait, one that forms an essential part of many a woman's self-description. But this approach, too, has to be subjected to the judgment seat of prudence. To move toward the extreme of self-effacement is as threatening to wholeness as the extreme of self-enhancement. Women need to find the middle way of moderation. Many have been caught in the grip of cultural pressures to succeed in a career, at times to the detriment of home and family life. Both retain high priority in the self-descriptions of Catholic women.

Young women in particular feel torn between their social activist tendencies and their desire to give quality time and attention to marriage and children. This tension is mounting in our day. I do not see an easy solution. Women are drawn into the struggle for social justice, which is also time- and energy-consuming. After assuring me that she hates injustice in any form and will do all she can to correct it, one of my associates said:

> I approach things I believe in or feel strongly about with intensity. When I plan projects or programs related to an issue that means a lot to me, . . . I usually find myself barreling along to see it through. Whether that's good or bad, I don't know. I'm known . . . as someone who gets things done. I try hard to be sensitive to the feelings of other people along the way. However, I do know not everybody is comfortable with my high intensity.

The ambiguity she feels about herself is evident. Cannot we identify with the dilemma of being unhappy if we work too intensely and hurt some people along the way, and being equally unhappy if we lay back and do not reach the goals we've set? Disentangling the dilemma would seem to suggest the need for self-discipline. To quote the same woman again:

> While I approach most of life with a lot of energy, I've found that I absolutely need time by myself to think and reflect on where my life is going. That time can be healing and invigorating. Unfortunately, it can also be associated with depression as I find myself filled with self-doubt, guilt, and the fear of not being accepted or liked.

Another familiar dilemma presents itself. On the one hand, this woman is certain about her need for oasis moments to restore the deeper "for what" of her life; on the other hand, she fears being perceived as out-of-it, as not so popular anymore. The question is: is she willing, as a Christian, to pay the price of being different or will she succumb to the pressure to conform to a functionalistic, performance-oriented society? This is the razor's edge along which many women walk. In some cases the inner tension between reclaiming one's ownmost self and having to prove oneself by means of high achievement is traceable to one's being raised in a dysfunctional family. As a child, a woman like this may have had a heavy load of responsibility thrust upon her — if, for example, either parent was alcoholic. Or she may have been sexually abused. It is beyond the scope of this book to treat such issues in depth. But I know that nothing can so crush and deform womanspirit than abusive or violent parents or their substitutes.

It is nothing short of amazing that so many women rise up from the ashes of these circumstances and create for themselves an ambiance of beauty and dignity. Some force propels women from within — the force of womanspirit. It is elusive yet elucidated, obscure yet obvious, quiet yet not willing to quit. It is one word that covers many experiences. Here is a sampling of answers I received to the question of what it means to be womanspirit in touch with the world:

> I, woman, am creative,
> > reflective,
> > introspective,
> > sensitive.

> I am an energetic worker,
> > president of many organizations,
> > an introvert, an extrovert.

> I have strong religious beliefs,
> and consider myself to be imaginative,
> > > intuitive,
> > > intelligent,
> > > sensitive,
> > > friendly and approachable,
> > > giving and usually pleasant.

> I, woman, read extensively, voraciously,
> > base my life on Christian principles,
> > travel, teach, knit, garden, sing,
> > play tennis, cook, paint, study nature.

I am active,
> responsible,
> dependable,
> prophetic,
> practical,
> independent in my thinking,
> persistent in my achievement of adopted goals.

I am persevering,
> conceptualizing,
> strategizing,
> efficient and motivated.

I am also warm and caring,
> involved and prayerful,
> joyful and full of fun.

I, woman, am loving and protective,
> intense, outrageous, audacious.

I think all the time.
I am dependable.
I am restless and dream-filled.
I am good.
I have a good heart.
I am a mother, a wife, a friend, a daughter.
I am alive.

I, woman, am not timid
> or afraid to speak out
> or to walk in front of the line.

I am seldom, if ever, totally predictable.
At times I try too hard to run the Lord's show.

I am self-confident,
> disciplined,
> competent,
> proud,
> impetuous,
> stubborn,
> strong-willed.

I, woman, know pain,
>> anxiety,
>> depression,
>> guilt,
>> sorrow,
>> and longing — for someone, for God.

I flow easily with the rhythms of the day,
> walking
> talking
> relating
> watching
> praying
> conversing
> sharing
> studying
> learning.

I am quickly drained,
> not enough alone,
> too busy,
> impatient,
> far from perfect,
> not letting God guide my life,
> wanting to let go,
> needing a hug,
> losing self-confidence,
> trying too hard.

I am wise,
> a natural leader,
> enthusiastic,
> a woman of faith,
> deeply religious,
> interested in people,
> attending to detail,
> respectful of the truth,
> serious and playful,
> passionate and cool,
> judgmental and merciful,
> courageous and cowardly,

flowing and rigid,
serious and shallow.

I am never bored.
I am nice, and gentle.
I am vulnerable.
I am a take-charge person.
I can be overly dependent, and independent.
I find people fascinating.
I have work to do.
I must not be wasted.
I am woman.

6 ❧

Women's Most Treasured Relationships

REFLECTING ON THE RESPONSES I received from Catholic women about the relationships they held most dear, I could see four categories emerging as basic: God, family members, friends, and community. It came as no great surprise that God is the center from whence all other significant relationships flow. This insight reminded me of a conversation I once had with a spiritual guide, who said to me in a gentle yet insistent way: "If you do not develop a person-to-person relationship with God — a real love relationship — you'll never be happy." I said, "Never sounds like a long time," and he replied, "So does 'forever,' and that's how long committed love lasts." Shortly thereafter, first for class preparation and then later for personal formation, I began reading the *Collected Works* of John of the Cross. When I read one of his sayings, I knew in my heart what the old priest was trying to tell me. With the certitude one would expect of a saint, this master of the spiritual life concludes: "At the evening of life, you will be examined in love. Learn to love as God desires to be loved and abandon your own ways of acting."

A relationship with God grows slowly and gradually over time as does the love between people. Love cannot be forced. It is like a plant exposed to sunshine. It blooms in due course provided someone waters and feeds it. A relationship requires dialogue and experienced intimacy. Little wonder, then, that the closest we come to knowing what God is like is to discover what it feels like to be loved by another person.

> Sometimes I think of God in an anthropomorphic way — experiencing God as Father, Brother, Lover, Friend, Teacher. At other times, God is more Mystery to me, yet Someone with whom I have a relationship, Ground of my being and source of strength and healing for me in a personal way.

God, as our Lover, is nearer to us than we are to ourselves, yet there always remains between us a residue of distance, a reminder that there is about true love a mystery no one can ever really fathom. Have you not felt at moments of closest intimacy a mysterious receding of the one you love? Have you not touched his or her face, traced the line from forehead to chin, and wondered, who is this person I love so much? How did he/she come to be? Why, out of all the others I could have met, are we here and now together? It feels as if breath itself will break the spell of intimacy. And, soon enough, with a stretch, a sigh, a yawn, life returns to its ordinary round. Yet who of us would want to miss such a moment? So it is with God.

Not to relate to God as our Lover would be to miss a powerful source of consolation. Prayer to me is this personal, involved way of relating to God. Without this closeness to the Divine Source of energy and light, to the Son (the Sun) of God, we would be less productive, less joyful persons.

> There have been times when I've felt convinced that were it not for the grace of God in my life, I would not only be unable to do the work I do; I would myself be clinically depressed.

If depression means feeling lost and lonely, lacking in purpose, too slothful to seize the moment, if depression is the tip of the iceberg of self-pity, resentment, and disillusionment, then depressed is what my life, too, would be without God. It is astounding that the Sacred can be so forgotten in our culture. It is as if spirituality, not sexuality or aggression, has become the repressed sector. Arrogance and self-aggrandizement replace humility and a sense of dependence on the forming mystery in whom we live and move and have our being (Acts 17:28). The truth is, in the words of two women:

> I treasure my relationship with God because without it *I* would be annihilated — not just dead. It is breath and life and force and blood and existence and eternity. Apart from God I am not. I am because God is. No other reason.
>
> •
>
> I owe my life — not just my afterlife, but my present, earthly existence to God. I am ... grateful for what God has done in my life already, amazed by what will be.

This is strong language, but it says, in effect, that we never want to treat lightly the sheer gift of being here ... in a woman's body, capable of generating new life in a variety of ways, aware as a Christian that the Word became flesh in Mary's womb, that Christ burst through cultural taboos and befriended women, making them his disciples.

I realize that my own faith is growing stronger every time I am aroused to awe by the sight of a sky splashed purple and pink by a tropical sunset. Sighs of gratitude escape my lips when I feel my mouth watering in anticipation of the first bite of freshly baked whole wheat bread. It becomes harder to hold back the tears that spill over with each swelling chord of Samuel Barber's symphony, *Adagio for Strings.*

We owe the God of love the love of God. Having been loved first by God, can we offer less than our whole heart? Dare we love others without loving our own most loveable selves? In the Great Commandment resides the double directive we need to follow to live always in appreciation and amazement: loving God and loving others as we love ourselves. Recognition of what matters most may be granted to us directly by God (witness Paul's turn around on the road to Damascus), but mostly the message of love comes from human mediation:

> A gifted counselor who not only prayed and cried for me but who risked being vulnerable taught me how to be human. It was the turning point in my life — the point at which I stopped being dead and began to live again and the point at which I received the greatest gift of all — my personal relationship with Jesus. I received acceptance and my identity.

I realize as I read this account of conversion that my own sense of acceptance, my awareness of who I am, has everything to do with my belief that I stand at all times before God. Before a word is on my lips, God knows the whole of it. I believe that God accepts me as I am and, therefore, that I can accept and appreciate myself. Self-appreciation is not a question of "me" autonomously giving credence to "my" self. I am too fragile, too imperfect, too human. It is a matter of believing with all my heart that God thinks the world of me. God made me, this unique self and no other. If God does not complain about a chipped mug, why should I?

My sense of identity is equally dependent on knowing that I am, before I become anything else, a child of God. God is my source, the ground out of which I emerge, the guide I can count on to lead me through a veritable valley of tears. I know that God sees me in ways I cannot see myself, and that what God beholds is good. For this reason I and many Christian women find ourselves talking to God on and off, all day long. God is for one woman "like a generator," the point of contact to replenish her energies and calm her worries. This energy analogy is one I frequently use and feel. Without daily times of in-touchness with the Sacred, I know my batteries would run low. I would risk becoming irritable and impatient. I would soon wilt like a plant without water. Why? That question was answered simply yet profoundly by one woman religious with whose insights many of us, myself included, would agree:

> For me, God is both inside of me and in all that is out-side of me, a part of and yet beyond, personal and yet an all-encompassing environment. Within recent years, I have experienced that there is "Someone" or "Something" very real, very strong both within and beyond me that is a pres-ence, a source, a sustainer, a call-er in my life. That presence is unbelievable, radically faithful, enduring deep underneath and beyond all the other relationships in my life. When this relationship became so powerful for me, I tended to attribute its strength to my celibate lifestyle. I have moved around a lot; have established deep relationships with both women and men, put a lot of energy into the continued growth of those relationships, communicated much about myself to those sig-nificant others, only to experience that often they lack the response that I had been hoping for or desiring. As a result, even as I continued to sustain those meaningful relationships,

I kept returning to "Someone" or "Something" deep within and beyond me as a source, a wellspring, of love, acceptance and challenge. I kept returning to God. Interestingly enough, I have found that I enter into other human relationships with a freedom from expectations that has allowed those to grow in a new way. I realize that no human relationship can fill the empty space, that lonely spot that longs for God. Consequently, I don't expect human relationships to do that: I can celebrate each one for what it is, for what we are to each other, knowing that the unfulfillment will be there until God comes. As a result, both my human relationships and my relationship with God have taken on a new beauty and meaning; I live in thankfulness for them all. I am also realizing that the fundamental loneliness I experience is not unique to me as a celibate woman; it is the human condition that provides space for God to long for us and for us to long for God. This has made me, as a woman religious, feel not separate from but a part of the human race of loving and being loved.

Family relationships are seen both as sources of joy and pain in the lives of the women I questioned. Parents, siblings, spouses, children, and other extended family members — aunts, uncles, nieces, nephews, grandparents — have a major role to play in the formation story of married and single women. Whether one's children are young or older, their well-being preoccupies a good parent. Whether the "kids" live at home or in another neighborhood, city, or state, their influence on the family and the family's influence on them is a binding force, for better or worse. "My family is important to me," said one single women, "so much so that, though I live far away, they are a part of who I am." I know that my own identity is inseparable from the initial formation I received at home: how I dress, what I like to eat, the customs I try to retain around the holidays, my taste in decor, my choice of car. In slight and significant ways, if I'm honest with myself, I detect traces of my upbringing at home.

Not surprisingly, of immense importance to women is their relationship with their mothers. When this tie is close, mothers would be described also as best friends; when the relationship is fraught with difficulties, there is no doubt that daughters suffer. Here are two revealing testimonies:

I have always had a close relationship with my mother. She has been hospitable to my friends. She and I have understood and enjoyed each other's humor. My mom raised four children while Dad was traveling on business; I appreciate her independence and competence. She — and her mother — have been the kind of women who take care of things, look after their families, and rarely complain. I wish I were more like them.

•

While I believe my relationships with family members were the most important and influential ones in my life, they were not the ones I've "treasured." They were far too painful. My relationship with my mother is strained. I love her, and I'm sure she loves me, but we are extremely different people. She has a hard time understanding why women would not want a traditional life in the home and, in many ways, devalues women. When I was growing up, she used to tell me that boys were better people and made better friends. . . . Perhaps hardest for me, she lives vicariously through me and has a hard time seeing where our lives and souls are different.

Whereas one mother-daughter bond gives life and generates healthy autonomy, the other drains energy and requires continual conditioning so that the daughter, in this case, can survive as an independent, mature woman in her own right. I would venture to say nothing so sustains a woman, psychologically and spiritually, than a mother who nurtures her but does not try to control her. By the same token, nothing is so depleting for a woman than to be in the clutches of a manipulative mother, who does not ask how her daughter feels or what she thinks but tells her exactly what she can and cannot do based on the myth that "Mother knows best." Sometimes that's true, but Mother is also a limited human being, who may herself be the victim of deformative parenting. The tactics of undercutting one's already fragile self-esteem, evoking "guilt trips," and subtly making children feel responsible for one's failures, for instance, in the area of substance abuse, are often passed on from one generation to the next in a dysfunctional family. When the atmosphere in the family is conducive to spiritual growth, then the outcome might sound something like this:

Needless to say I treasure my relationship with my mother and father. Their wisdom, faith, and guidance have helped me as a wife, mother, and friend. I feel close to my friends and my sister because of our deep faith in God, a faith passed on to us through our education by good parents. We find joy in everyday events and share mutual longings for things spiritual.

I mentioned the special place grandparents may play in one's familial formation. I was happy to learn that I am not alone in feeling grateful for a grandmother's sustaining love. The following memories of one woman's childhood evoke my own flashbacks as I recall that sweet interlude between innocence and experience. At the age of nine or ten, I distinctly remember wanting to stop time and stand forever secure under the strong arms of my maternal grandmother, a woman who saw life in the raw and still reeled with laughter. As an adult, long after her death, I was finally able to absorb the sober truth she knew so well — that we only have one life to live, and it is foolhardy not to make the best of it.

My maternal grandmother has always been especially important to me. She, more than anyone, gave me unconditional love while I was growing up. She babied me, while my mother was rushing me to grow up before the two brothers and sisters behind me. I spent much time with Grandma. She taught me how to plant a garden, how to peel apples and bake a pie, how to drink my tea and milk out of a saucer. (But don't let your parents see you doing this!) She told me family stories and showed me baby bunnies in the garden. In high school, she hemmed my skirts as short as I wished (it was the style) and listened without criticism or direction while I talked about boys. She always had time to visit, and my friends enjoyed her, too. When I went off to college, she regularly sent mail, and always included a couple of dollars for treats. We shared secrets. I loved her quick, irreverent sense of humor, her kindness and earthiness. When, in her seventies, she became more and more ill, I quit my job to take care of her with my aunt and mother. I was able to tell her that I hoped I would be the kind of grandmother to my grandchildren that she had been to me. Writing this brings tears to my eyes. I miss her. She is woven into the fabric of who I am. She was a dear friend to me.

Recalling my own good fortune in this regard made me all the more appreciative of the evidence I saw of friendship between young and old when I visited Africa for the first time in the summer of 1984. In the villages and townships in South Africa, Kenya, and Tanzania, the sites of our lecture schedule, it was obvious that old ones are venerated — never, but never, "farmed out." A retirement home for the elderly would be unthinkable in that part of the world. Elderly people bridge the gap between the ancestors and this generation. They are story tellers, the bearers of tradition. The young, with eager eyes and courteous expectancy, would gather around the table and listen to legends that took on new meaning each time they were unfurled. One of the times I cherish most from that tour was a trip to the hometown of a student, a priest of the diocese of Moshi, whose parents were celebrating their forty-eighth wedding anniversary. I can still taste the banana beer they offer honored guests and smell the meat roasting on an open fire. All ages mingled. The air tingled with tales of olden days. Laughter flowed like rippling water softening the jagged edges of a nearby brook. The veneration shown to the old couple was a memorable sight to behold. It made me feel humble. I could not hold a candle to the faith of these village people. This is a partial recollection of that day from the journal I kept:

> We drove along the clay-packed rocky "main" road until we came to what looked like a grass covered driveway at which point Father R. turned in and announced that we had entered his neighborhood, the village of Kyou, and, indeed, if one peered through the banana trees, the coffee bean trees, the corn and vegetables, at the end of small paths there were the tin roofed cement or wooden houses and huts in which the whole community lived, recreated, worked, prayed, and shared life fully from sunrise to sunset. We parked the car at the end of the "main street" in what Father called his "garage," an open matted spot, and began the walk down to his parents' home along a steep footpath past banana trees and in view of the cultivated slopes characteristic of the hill country south of Kilimanjaro.

Minutes later, we made our way down the last steps of the hillside to the small patio where awaiting us with cups of banana beer and garlands of flowers were the honored couple, mother in yellow print, father in a dark brown suit. We greeted them in the few Kiswahili words we knew and participated in the welcoming ritual of exchanging sips of beer.

Father R. told us that the faith of his parents, once they converted, could not be stifled, for it was rooted in an awed presence to the Sacred, who speaks in these mystical hills and valleys to the hearts of gentle people like his parents.

A delicious odor of roast pork filled the air. We were invited to move from the porch to the living room where Father R.'s parents, relatives, and guests were waiting. On the table in a large tray was the roasted half pig, the main dish of a wonderful feast. Eating would commence in a ritual way after the speeches — one welcoming us on behalf of the family, another expressing Father R.'s personal gratitude to his parents. We learned later that his father and mother carried him on their backs when he was a tall, sturdy fourteen-year-old, terribly ill, to a doctor who saved his life. Though we could not understand every word of the story and thanks he expressed, by watching the faces of his parents, we knew what his address meant to them in their old age.

Tears welled up in our eyes in the presence of these faithful Christians. Holy pictures and posters graced the walls of their simple abode. The air purred with the sound of blessings and prayers. Then Father R. sliced into the meat and served a piece to his father who received it on his tongue, as if it were communion; the same ritual was repeated for his mother. Then the entire assembly burst into applause, and the feast began in full. Life might be difficult, but today the sheer power of the human spirit, inspired by the Holy Spirit, ensured survival.

At day's end, laughing and by candlelight, we were led in the near dark back to the car. Night fell on an unforgettable day. In this part of the world, there is neither electricity nor running water, truly no modern conveniences as we in the West know them, yet the people are happier than many we saw in the bigger towns. St. Paul's words suddenly played in my mind: "For the foolishness of God is wiser than human wisdom, and the weakness of God is stronger than human strength" (1 Cor. 1:25), as well as Jesus' own prayer: "I give you praise Father, Lord of heaven and earth, for although you have hidden these things from the wise and the learned you have revealed them to the childlike" (Lk. 10:21).

When a respectful relationship grows between husband and wife over many years, their marriage, as a local saying suggests, is like a garden. The strength of their commitment is the soil into which are sown seeds of harmony and accord that bear fruit in the family. Their togetherness, to paraphrase the poet Rilke, is not a question of creating quick community by tearing down and destroying all boundaries but a covenant guaranteeing that each appoints the other guardian of his or her solitude. With God at the center of their life and love, the couple promises with the greatest degree of confidence to care for one another exclusively and faithfully until death. It is as if one says to the other, "I will you to be in fidelity to your unique life call." The communion they enjoy, the community that emerges as a by-product of their love and grace, transcends vitalistic crowds or functionalistic teams. Their side-by-sideness is romantic and realistic; their family ambiance is affective and effective; their faith in one another and in God is strong enough to resist the ebbing tides of success and failure, health and sickness, life and death. Whether a woman communicates her feelings in an African village or an American suburb, her sense of what makes a marriage work is the same:

> My husband and I have always done almost everything together — worked in a medical field, participated in outside activities, continued weekly Mass together since Day One. I respect him, am proud of him, and trust his love for me.

A good marriage, women responded, moves through a number of stages. The first involves letting go of one's independence while simultaneously learning to become interdependent. Simply put, this means living and working under one roof — sharing the same bed, eating meals together, struggling to raise a family, getting past disruptive outbursts, never going to sleep angry — the list of everyday challenges is endless. One of the hardest lessons to learn, by women's own admission, is total acceptance of one another, especially when opinions differ and conflicts disrupt anticipated tranquility.

Fighting over the smallest things — like where to keep an extra set of car keys — can raise one's defenses to the status of full alert. Day by day, if love deepens despite setbacks on the plane of personality differences, there grows between two people the special grace of intimacy. A friend once defined this term by means of the wordplay: *into me see*. We need someone who knows us through and through and still wants to be with us. A wife wants a husband to feel that living with her is worth the risk of occasional anger, the menace of misunderstanding. The transformation of conflict from a competitive contest to a creative chance to learn more about one another is a goal worth pursuing. In the end, fidelity depends on the willingness to surrender in marriage to one another and to God. Then real care emerges — not phony sweetness that may mask a lie, but true love.

> My relationship with my husband is my most important earthly one. My picture of P. and me is that he is an enormous rock on the beach and I am a kite, sailing on unlimited string because one end is tied around the rock. I anguish over letting P. have the place in my life that only God should occupy. If P. died, the string would be severed and I would literally feel as if I were lost from the face of the earth, lost in space. It terrifies me — this kind of love — and yet I know I would survive. Love holds you, but it also lets you stand on your own two feet.

Lest one idealize marital love, it is necessary to understand what intense labor a marriage demands. It is in this sense a vocation, a serious commitment calling upon every physical, mental, emotional, and spiritual resource one has. There are crosses to bear every day, beginning with growing accustomed to one another's ingrained habits and "morning to evening" rituals. Women whose marriages have lasted tell me that it takes hard work, both before and after children come along. Quality time together in today's fast-paced world tends to drain away like water in an unplugged tub. Scheduling alone calls for heroic efforts when both parents work. But to come through the hard years of initial sharing and childrearing and still be one another's best friend is no small feat.

I am always amazed and edified by what God and a good couple can do to make life not only bearable but beautiful for many. If we have been fortunate enough to grow up in a loving family, with strong religious roots, we have a better chance of making it through the tremors of adolescence and growing into mature adults. "There is a bond in family that has for me the steadfastness of no other human relationship," one woman said. This truism may explain why so many women of faith believe in and do all they can to support family life.

> As I grow older I treasure my family more and more. Knowing that we will not live under one roof forever prompts us to try to appreciate to the full what we have now and who we are to each other.

This investment of time and energy in spouse and children is both draining and rewarding, as this mother admitted:

> Together with my relationship with my husband, my children teach me what unconditional love means, and it is like dying. It is painful, but it is real. I said to the Lord once, "I'd like to know what *agapic* love is," and I said to him once more, "Teach me to really love." And he showed me that love is how we work out our salvation in our state of life and that is why I am committed — for life.

Women describe their children as gifts, "each one unique and fascinating." Admittedly, it is easy in the throes of daily living to lose sight of the transcendent horizon that there is more to life that diaper-changing, than cooking, cleaning, and slaving away in and outside the home. What helps is an inner conversion process that changes routine chores into avenues for contemplation. Hence one woman confirmed that the "spirituality of diaper-changing" is what enables her to find deeper meaning in the mundane passing of the day. Looking back on the years spent in acts of self-giving and in watching her girls grow, this mother comes to the sudden self-discovery:

> I cannot think about life without them. In many ways, they gave birth to me. . . . They have also altered ALL of my plans for my life. They sometimes need *me* too much and I like that too much. They are a care. They have taxed everything in me.

They show me the best in me and the worst. They love me. I have been so strong (such a force in their lives) that my final gift to them will be, perhaps, that only in my death will they really live — Oh, dear, that sounds too dramatic. It's time to stop and do the dishes and get my feet back on the ground.

There is nothing like a family to pull one back to earth. When the "what could be's" threaten to cut us off from reality, a dripping nose, a soccer game on a wet field, a birthday cake that has to be picked up NOW! communicate the "what is" that roots spirituality in reality, in the Nazareth of everydayness, in "scouts, altar boy practice, school plays, music and dance lessons, sports, volunteer lunch programs, and all that comprises whatever it means, in the words of Walter Ciszek, S.J., 'to engineer your life in the Lord.'"

Women admit that they would be lost without the support of friends who are other than family members. In fact, friendship surfaced as a central concern for married and single women. In addition, a special place was accorded to community, especially in the lives of women religious. Community, they said, must allow room for diversity. True community does not squelch creativity by mandating uniformity. It is not a crowd or a collectivity but a place where people can expend their knowledge and experience of self, others, and God.

> I treasure my religious congregation because it is here, along with my sisters, that I have also matured and learned much about myself, and what the living of religious life entails. I've learned a lot about women, too. Some are more valiant and grace-full than others, but, however unique we may be, we are called to live and share a communal life.

For many the church community offers a "sense of family," a gathering of unique believers who share common joys and sorrows and a firm commitment to Christ. What women cared most about were "heart friends," other women and men, relatives or not, whose trust had passed the test of time.

> I've known a few of my friends since high school, a few from my years as a young single woman, and several now in my roles as wife, mother, and volunteer. I also have older friends of both sexes. They have all brought something unique and beautiful into my life. Some I admire for their abilities in areas

into which I would only dream of venturing; others have similar lifestyles but show me new ways of looking at and dealing with our shared interests and concerns.

Friends were named "treasures of love" by many. I thank God daily for those few special relationships in my own life that are the lifelines that bail me out of bad times. To have someone with whom to laugh and cry, to speak and be silent, is a gift I would not trade for gold. But we take a risk. I have been burnt once or twice by trusting too lightly. I have been betrayed, and that hurts badly. The answer is not to withdraw to a safety zone of noninvolvement. Nor is it to live in the bargain basement of "I'll do for you if you do for me." Trial and error applies as much to friendship as to a new business venture.

Some relationships work out; others have to be unstitched. It is no one's fault. Sometimes we outgrow each other or, maybe, we refuse to let go of our romantic illusions about the friend we want her or him to be. We build up expectations the other can never reach. When the bridge between us crumbles, we feel betrayed. Who is to blame? More often than not, we refused to read the signs posted along the way. Not every relationship into which we enter can last. Lifelong friendships are among life's rarest gems.

> In the case of my closest friend, we have both suffered personal tragedy and were of great support to each other in those experiences. The fact is, we've been friends for almost twenty-five years, and we still have to work at having our relationship grow and deepen while being able to form friendships with others in our lives.

We may find a few friends like this, with the grace of God, but mostly we enjoy temporary companions who ease the way without feeling the need to follow us to the end of the road. Luckily, for us, God never turns back. Love accompanies us all the way home. Every time we move, we have to make new friends. It helps to know that one Friend goes with us wherever we are.

We meet people at work, in parishes, at social gatherings. With any one of them, we may strike up a friendship. We may even meet that person with whom we can share our life platonically or in a Christian marriage. For one unmarried woman of my acquaintance, the tie that binds her relationship with her boyfriend is chastity.

She admits it is "nearly a phenomenon in the American dating culture of the 1990s when uninhibited sexual expression, despite the threat of AIDS and other sexually transmitted diseases, is on the rise among young people of all populations." For this woman and for many whose faith is based on a person-to-Person relation with God, "the chaste expression of love reflects respect . . . mirrored in compassion, concern, and in love for one another." By preserving the sexual expression for marriage, she feels she is saying to her friend: "I care more about who you are than what you can do for me or how you can make me feel."

Friendship ranges the spectrum from casual and passing to serious and lasting, but through these changes Christ stands at the center. His love is everlasting. When we allow his grace to fill the fragile vessel of human relationships, its power will spill over into our working world and social encounters. Chaste, respectful love will not remain a lofty ideal but will become a living reality.

> Even if I disagree with someone on the job or at a social function, before reacting too sternly, I try to restrain my tongue from critical, verbal lashing of the one with whom I disagree. I challenge myself in this way not only to preach but to practice the Golden Rule, loving others as I love myself because God loves me.

I have learned through reading and shared reflection that in many ways relationships are what keep women anchored to others and to God. "They are my gravity . . . they are what I am about." As to which of these are most treasured, the list reads like a litany. I, woman, thank God for:

My grandparents
Two elderly women babysitters
A gifted counselor
My husband
My children
A confessor
My best friend
My mother and my father
My brothers
A special baby sister
Our parish priest

The women religious with whom I live
My nieces and nephews
A few close male friends
The neighborhood dry cleaner
My Bible study group
The choir members
My grandchildren
My neighbor, who opened my eyes to the spirit
A priest and family friend, who said all will be well if Jesus is
    at the center of my life
My church
My closest female friend
Members of my religious congregation
Members of the National Black Sisters Conference, who
    champion the cause of minority women
Strong women, who are leaders and have helped me to grow,
    women who stand up for what they believe in and who
    are ready to fight the good fight
My boyfriend
The saints
Two women friends
Creatures in nature, great and small
(And at the heart of love)
Christ Jesus, revealed to us as fully human and fully divine,
    as prophet and brother, mediator and master, the Messiah,
    who taught us to love one another as he loved us because
    we are his friends (Jn. 15:12–15).

When I ask myself how I know I believe, I have no satisfactory answer at all, no assurance at all, no feeling at all. I can only say with Peter, Lord I believe, help my unbelief. And all I can say about my love of God is, Lord help me in my lack of it. I distrust pious phrases, particularly when they issue from my mouth. I try militantly never to be affected by the pious language of the faithful but it is always coming out when you least expect it. In contrast, to the pious language of the faithful, the liturgy is beautifully flat.
— *Flannery O'Connor*

Formative Influences
on Women of Faith

DISEMBARKING AT THE AIRPORT in Memphis, Tennessee, I remembered that my secretary had warned me not to be upset by the directions I would find in my travel folder. I was on my way to a small town south of the city where I was scheduled to address an interfaith assembly. She added, almost as if apologizing, that she had transcribed the information verbatim as dictated by one of my hosts.

Already late for six o'clock supper, I rushed through the car rental procedure, informed the clerk that I did not need a map, found my vehicle, and headed south. Once away from the airport, I pulled over to the side of the road, as was my custom, and only then read the directions. No wonder she was worried. I was being told to "meander south a bit" until I saw an old farmhouse "bent down like a lame goat, . . . " hold a steady course south, then watch for a "big oak tree" — best slow down here "cause right past it was the first left . . . but don't yo'all fret 'cause soon enough there'd be a right pretty red barn set on a hill but don't yo' bother 'bout that 'cause up a piece was the next right.... "

After twenty minutes into this "sure short cut" to the conference center, I was unabashedly lost. The supper hour had come and gone and I was growing more nervous as the sun began to set. Forsaking all stubbornness, I stopped at the next gas station — really a ramshackle office with one pump outside, but, thank goodness, a light was burning in the window. Desperate for directions, I stormed in, thoroughly distraught. There behind the counter was a Buddha-like, pot-bellied old codger who looked to me as if he had been rocking back and forth in the same wicker chair for thirty or so years. Printout in hand, I blurted out my frustration with these southern-style directions. "Could you give me some clue as to where I am? ... I hate driving in a strange place in the dark ... I'm late for dinner ... I've never been so lost in my life" ... and on and on with my city slicker complaints. All the old badger did was rock and listen, chewing his cigar, unflapped by my consternation. Only when I ran out of breath did he look up at me with all-knowing eyes and shake his head. Then he told me in words I'll never forget: "Honey ... you ain't lost ... you're here ... and there ain't no way you can be lost if yo're here."

It was as if "God" had spoken. Right. How could I be lost if I was here? How could any of us be lost if we are where God calls us to be? The old man's insight hit home. He became a kind of icon of formation wisdom. His remark still manages to calm me when I'm running in a thousand different directions like a "blind pig." Every time it seems as if I'm losing my way, I remember that the race does not always belong to the swift, that it is good to slow down and smell the roses. I had lost my flow with the day and the night and the seasons. The answer was not to seek directions from outside but to look at what I was doing to myself within. If I lost my center in God, then I was really a goner. The old man gave me a spiritual secret money could not buy: be present where you are, where God places you, and you can never be lost.

The last rays of the sun were fading from the horizon, the sky was awash with pink and purple hues of summer, when I left the station. Calmly, as if he had all the time in the world, my pot-bellied Buddha drew me a map I could understand. He assured me I could find my way, even in the dark. And I did. I arrived in time to enjoy southern fried catfish, corn fritters, and crisply minted ice tea. I should have known that dinner does not need to start on time in the South for people to have a good time.

Many people, events, and things pass in and out of our lives, making no noticeable difference. Only a few manage to stand out in memory. These comprise an unforgettable series of vignettes, a collection of narratives passed around like a beloved photograph album. These are what count as truly influential. Birth and death, youth and aging, happenings at home, at church, in school, encounters with old and new friends — any of these may make their mark upon us. As much as we might like to think of ourselves as free spirits, we are the products of the people who touch us, the places we have been, the traditions we pass on. Our lives are, and are not, our own. Weddings and funerals, for instance, ignite the "when I was" and "wish you could have seen me then" remembrances that our children's children still narrate.

When I asked women what they remembered as one of, if not *the*, most formative influence in their life, one went back in memory to the nursing school in Washington, D.C., where she developed for the first time her sense of independence, her industry and devotion to the sick. Another recalled the first meeting, the exact moment, when she accepted that her husband was an alcoholic. I learned in due course that she had been brought up in a Lutheran church but had grown away from the practice of religion. Then this event occurred:

> When I was expecting our first child, I started thinking about the religious training I wanted for him or her and thought it would be best if both my husband and I became Catholics. So when my daughter was baptized I was confirmed. Yet it was not until attending AA meetings, reading the literature, and talking about the program with my husband that I began to feel in touch with God, with the desire to have God be the Guide of our life.... I now have the wherewithal to return to church with a new appreciation for what my faith offers.

I often repeat to myself the familiar saying, because it applies so well: "God writes straight with crooked lines." God has a way of leading us where at first we would not go. When we pause to remember who we are and the way in which the mystery has brought us to this place, do we not see the thin red line of divine providence trailing its way through the turns on the road? Some people seem to appear when we need them the most. We have little or no say in the matter. When our inner control tower experiences a power failure, that is when, to quote my mechanically minded brother, the divine generator kicks in. When we run out of excuses for hiding from God, we can ask ourselves the risky question: "What is my heart telling me to do?" The answer is simple: "Go where God is leading." Then we can assess and be challenged by, we can celebrate and flow with, the events and experiences of each day.

It is here that God speaks to us and we speak to God. It is now out of which and into which everything else flows. Learning to be present where we are is energizing. Resting for a while in our self-chosen oasis enables the eternal to slip through the temporal like thread through a needle. The pressures of work recede like ebbing waves into the wide reaches of the sea. We behold a tinge of forever in the ticking hands of life's relentless clock. Surely these times of slowing down allow the best that is in us to take a breather.

Once, traveling by plane across the country from Pittsburgh to San Diego, I sat beside a handsome — by his own description — "high roller," a man in his forties, wealthy, twice married, twice divorced. He said, after I introduced myself as a teacher of formative spirituality, that we had nothing in common. Still, as is often the case in a transcontinental encounter between strangers who will most likely never meet again, we embarked upon an animated conversation. His interests centered on gambling, golf, sport fishing, entertainment, gourmet cooking, and, of course, beautiful women "with great legs." I said that his life sounded rather one-sided to me. Did he ever think about anything besides his own pleasures? Taken aback, he described how over the past fifteen years the women he had known were, like him, looking for two things: fun and money. "I never know if they like me or only what I can buy for them." Not knowing what to say, I almost ended the exchange there and went back to my book. Still, since we had three more hours of flight time to go, I ventured one more question: "Do you ever take time to get in touch with yourself or is it always go, go, go?"

I must have touched the right chord with that one because he began a searching explanation of his life story while I listened. He told of loves won and wasted; business ventures begun and collapsed to pay debts and amass capital; a first wife loved and lost because of his own infidelity; a second spouse married for business reasons, but no children. He never did things in moderation: "I

have to be flying high or brought low." "Is there any in-between,"
I asked, "any time when you feel really together?" He recalled a
time a few years ago when he took a ten-day island vacation. "It
took me at least three days to get to the edge of 'being normal.'
By the last day I began to have some sense of myself . . . then I got
scared and had to pick up the phone — I do that a lot because I'm
afraid of being alone." "What do you want most out of life?" was
the last question I posed before the four scotches he had gulped
down put him to sleep. "To be loved by a good woman."

Here was a man who by the look of him — designer shoes, a
diamond-studded watch, a silk shirt — had it all, yet by his own
admission, he was alone and unhappy. At one point in our banter I described to him a scene in the bar of a fashionable Palm
Beach hotel that left an imprint on my mind. The setting was serene
and sophisticated. A long, low window stretched the length of the
room. Flowing toward it was a sweep of the Atlantic Ocean looking
as if it were within arm's reach. Everyone was dressed to the hilt —
"Guccied out," as I remarked to my companion. Their faces, mirrored over the bar, were hang-dog unhappy, their eyes glazed over
with booze and boredom, their laughter high-pitched but lacking
humor.

Here were pleasure, power, and possession aplenty. I saw no
abandoned bodies, only a bar full of abandoned souls. I felt a wave
of pity for each person there. They were so richly attired and so poor
in spirit. Trust in transcendence, a sense of the "More Than," was
eroded by a passion for immediacy. Meditation on life's meaning
was the missing link.

When my traveling companion woke up, he said he had had a
series of strange dreams, sparked no doubt by our conversation. His
head hurt. It was the first time in months he had thought seriously
about himself and he thanked me for caring enough to draw him
into a real conversation. I imagined for one minute what it would
have been like to step behind that bar, take a cake of Ivory Soap,
and write on the flawless mirror, "So what?" I settled instead for
a short prayer: "Thank you, Holy Mystery, for teaching me the
lesson that having does not make one happy." Being whole, being
loved, helping others — these are the keys to consonance.

The persons with whom I live and minister have always been
the most formative influence in my life. I believe that maturity

> in formation is a result of being open to and accepting of the needs, manner of living, and outlook of those with whom I daily come in contact, while at the same time retaining the truth of my own personality — a concept spoken of well by Shakespeare: "To thine own self be true...."

The way to wholeness is not shaved as smoothly as a slide. It is often as pock-marked and hazardous as the roads of my city after the ravages of winter. There are potholes and ruts everywhere. Hub caps go flying hour by hour, making my hillside alone a junk collector's haven. The influences that shape a life are fraught with suffering. We tend to remember times of trauma and terror more than those of peace and joy.

> We never set a date for a wedding, but we both knew that when we were ready we would marry.... We had been together for over four years when my friend committed suicide.

In the face of cruel and sudden death, this woman endured months of nightmares. Her confidence in herself was shaken to the core; it was as if she could no longer count on her inner capacity for healing. The suicide of her beloved smashed her world, shattered her beliefs, left her "terrifyingly vulnerable." What happened could be compared to a sculptor crafting an exquisitely detailed hand only to destroy it in a fit of despair. The choice for her was either to remain forever in mourning or to move "slowly toward the possibility that there might be a God out there, something to make sense out of the chaos." Now the Master Artist became her teacher.

> God graciously waited upon me to come and then clearly taught me, encouraged me, showed me what was expected of me. I moved closer to the center in overlapping stages, to God as Creator-Artist, Teacher, Brother, Father, Beloved, Feminine Spirit, Ground of my being. And I experienced emotional healing — not just over this loss, but in other areas of my life as well. Where I had drifted before, I began to find clear direction. Work became ministry. Meditation became prayer. Out of the most difficult event in my life came the most precious gift, my relationship with God. Out of that emotionally crippling nightmare came a reflective understanding of pain

that would contribute later to the development of my career in psychology.

Women struggle to find meaning in what appears to be the antithesis of sense-making. Turning misery into ministry is an oft-repeated outlet. Doing something creative like painting or writing poems or books is another way of working through a deforma-tive influence. Scars caused by bad parenting slice into a woman's psyche and wound her world.

> I'm still trying to work through the anger of being sexually abused, of coming from a family with a history of schizophre-nia, of drug and alcohol addiction. Emotionally I had to raise myself. I have spent most of my life fighting depression. I cannot tell you how many psychotherapists, physicians, and representatives of the Catholic church I have seen since child-hood who virtually ignored my cries for help. Finally I found a therapist, not surprisingly a woman, who has been sensitive enough to recognize my hurt and to help me work through it.

While this woman's specific set of dehumanizing experiences may be unique, her story has been told by thousands of abused women. Her anger is legion. Women have been and are — in ris-ing numbers — victims of violent crime and every form of abuse. From exploitation in the media to lashings in our own living rooms, women suffer from the sins of sexism common in our society. For some this putdown begins already in childhood. One woman ad-mits that her parents were obstacles in her life more than good influences. "They were 'will-breakers' and my task became to dis-avow them entirely." She does not take pride in this willfulness, but it was necessary for her survival as a person under pressure. She compares her life to a castle under siege. She, the princess, had to become a skillful defender of her secret treasure, her inner life, which formidable tyrants tried to steal by subtle tactics that reduced her self-confidence She is a woman who was not raped physically but psychologically. She, too, had to turn to God for help. She had to find a way to entrust her will to God in an act of single-minded surrender while remaining strong enough to defend her integrity. The fine line between letting go and holding on to who she is often blurs. To complicate matters, she is trying to raise children who desire, as much as she did, to make their own decisions. Often she finds herself thinking against her better judgment, "No one else could possibly know how they should do things better than I!" No wonder life at times becomes too much for her and the children. That's when she remembers that even "Atlas needs to shrug!"

We women often try too hard to make things right. I know in my own life how often I have to lower the volume on "Control Center Me." As the movie *Steel Magnolias* portrays so powerfully, the spines of strong women stand straight, but if they become too brittle they will break. The mother in one symbolic scene rigidly controls her emotions when her daughter dies of kidney failure. She is able to keep the straitjacket on until everyone leaves the cemetery. Only when her friends challenge her composure does she break down completely and wail with grief.

No parent, no church, no society will ever be perfect. No marriage will go unscarred by misunderstanding. No friendship is ever entirely freed from bouts of betrayal. Life is a struggle from morning to night. The beauty is, we do not have to toss and turn alone. We are not trapped by circumstances. We are creatures drawn upward by God's transforming love, by touches of tender mercy. These are not pious imaginings but part of women's testimony to that which has the power to take mere clay and form it into a divine creation. We are, as Paul says, treasures in earthen vessels (2 Cor. 4:7).

> I see in myself the handiwork of God...

> ...love seems to cut through conflicts, challenges, disasters and augment understanding....

> Daily life amid woes and cares reminds me ever more of my need for God....

> I lose my footing when I neglect my prayer time. It is as if I almost need crises to jolt me back to the reality that I depend on God for all things.

Seeing in obstacles opportunities for ongoing formation is a gift of grace. Catholic women credit their faith for granting them this wider vision. Many acknowledge that the education they received in Catholic schools has been a mainstay through all the ups and downs of life.

> Most of what is really meaningful to me, my relationships, my thoughts about life, death, morality, my love of nature

and travel, work, pleasure have all been fostered and formed by my tie to the church.

The message of God's goodness buoys women up in the tempest-tossed unpredictability of daily life. Examples of believing parents, friends, teachers, and co-workers, who not only preach about but practice their faith, sustain women in times of crisis.

> My eighty-four-year-old friend is a spiritual prayer partner and a special pathway to God for me. Her West Indian wisdom is surely that of Solomon and she has the tenacity of St. Paul. Each conversation is like a homily wished for at Sunday Mass.... My family has given me a strong spiritual upbringing too. Through them I have come to realize that we are bound together as a people by a force greater than ourselves. Our black heritage is a kinship shared by and with the women of the church as we live our story and follow our journey and continue to believe in each other.

These stirring words remind me that the most formative influence we can name is, as one woman said, "Life itself." The people who cross the stage on which our all too short script unfolds are God's heralds. Do we listen to what the Holy Spirit attempts to tell us through them? Events that occur are not merely haphazard happenings that hang together like loose sand. They are part of a pattern, pieces in a providential picture the discerning eye can see. Do we behold the hand of God in everyday crises and their resolutions or have we lost our transcendent perspective in a flurry of efficient functioning and irresponsible pleasure seeking? Things do not belong to us like collectibles in a garage sale. Every one of them from the rug underfoot to the rain on the sill is a gift of God. Do we see ourselves as stewards appointed by our Creator to tend this fragile planet and use wisely its natural resources? Do we treat earth's limits with ecological sensitivity or think only of economic gain?

These are the kinds of questions we women are discussing among ourselves and before community boards and legislative bodies. Images of unifying and nurturing are surpassing those of dividing and conquering. Women are becoming outspoken critics of what is life-denying. We are sharing our feelings and views on morality and spirituality in a variety of forums. We value open exchanges between extremes on the left and the right, seeking avenues of reconciliation that are growth-producing for both parties.

Whatever else might be going on in this time of transition in the church, of this we can be certain: women's voices are being heard. Our influence will make a difference. Womanspirit has been awakened to the forming, reforming, and transforming power of God's word. This spirit, once released, will not again be contained. Womanspirit intends to usher the entire church into a new era of hope and reconciliation, an era refined, as might be expected, in crucibles of suffering and pain.

The humble can never rank God high enough nor themselves low enough. But here is the wonder: their weakness turns into wisdom, and the imperfection of their acts, always insufficient in their eyes, will be the greatest delight of their life.
— *Elizabeth of the Trinity*

8 ❧

Wisdom Women Want to Share

LESSONS FOR LIFE learned by my mother from her mother were passed on to me by way of several proverbs that bear repeating: "You have to share a ton of salt with someone before you know them"; "Save string because you never know what need tomorrow will bring"; "If you want something done properly, ask a busy person." Each generation wants to hand on to the next homey advice that teaches us more than long exhortations.

Life is a series of stories. Sometimes in the seemingly insignificant encounters who we are is being disclosed. On the eve of my mother's eightieth birthday, we were watching an old Garbo movie on cable TV. We were staying in an apartment in a small town on the Jersey shore where we had vacationed with the family for many years. Part of our weeklong celebration would be a surprise party on the actual day of her birth when my brothers and their families would join us, bringing along more food and gifts. I had in the meantime put together a slide presentation covering the past thirty years of our family's history. It would be another opportunity for all of us, especially the children, to learn our story. I had seen myself in the slides as a teenager, a college student, a European traveler, a journalist, a teacher. I was in places and with people I remembered vividly or hardly at all. Photos capture moments too precious to relinquish, too poignant to forget.

"It passes so quickly," she said to me. "How did eighty years go by already?"

"Even at my age, I know what you mean. One day it's Easter, the next, Christmas is here."

"There is one thing, though, I'll never understand."

"What's that?"

"Why can I remember every scene from this movie and not what I ate this morning or the appointments I have to keep. Between us, it's embarrassing. It makes me feel old. My life runs before me like the scenes of a picture show. I can still see us at the dinner table during the depression pretending that dandelions were a delicacy of the well-to-do."

"I hear it's a normal part of the aging process — a loss of surface memory. It's not serious. You're a goldmine of history. Who cares about this morning's meal. Tell me more about the Great Depression. Those must have been dark days...."

"You bet they were.... We had to work hard to eat, but that never killed anyone. Coffee cost a nickel, but three or four of us would have to pitch in to buy a seventy-five cent bun.... For some the depression meant going broke and starting over again; for others it destroyed their spirit.... Are you sure you want me to go on?"

"Yes, please. After all, how can I discover my story if I don't know yours?"

During this week of sharing many facts, the history of my origins fell into place. I not only filled in some of the memory blanks; I also realized from whence I derived the vital drive to bring a task, once started, to completion. My love for reading was no longer a mystery. My mother wanted a formal education in the worst possible way. Denied this chance because of her gender, she read "everything I could lay my hands on, and I read constantly to you, too." I caught the spirit of a woman whose love for life, whose aesthetic sensitivity, could turn a drab room into an attractively decorated dwelling in a flash of rearrangement and creative ingenuity.

This week of reminiscence helped me to reenter the recesses of my heart, where old loves and old hates still linger. In the atmosphere of recollection we created in our home away from home by the sea, I found myself remembering boy and girl friends I had not thought about for years; teachers and co-workers who caused me nothing but trouble and those without whom I could not have survived the vicissitudes of a challenging career. I knew that somewhere in the ebb and flow of my everydays I had come to a clearer understanding of what I believed in and why.

Mother said, "You have to know the few things for which you are willing to live or die." These essentials do not belong to any one of us alone; they are the whys of living we must take to heart and pass on to others. It was fascinating to hear the stories attached to the slides that appeared on the screen. "When did you plant that tree? Why were you laughing? Whose hand are you holding?" Each question peeled away one more layer of life. The power of narrative lifted us beyond the limits of the moment as we glimpsed the canvas upon which youth and age blend into one composite portrait.

Someone like Mother, who has had the luxury of living for many years, is able to tell us where we fit in the line of our relations. We can see in facial features and familiar traits why we behave as we do, from whence comes our preferences for certain foods, and why we want to feel as free to argue with the ones we love as to kiss and make up. During that week, I began to recover the origin of some of my own hopes and dreams. I thought again of the promises I had made to myself and to my God. I became, for whatever reason, more ready than ever to throw myself into the adventure of living. I began to accept realistically what could be accomplished in one lifetime and to let go of what was not meant to be.

"There is never enough time to do all that we want to do. There are never enough hours in the day to see the places we want to see and meet the people we want to meet. You can read the limits in the lines on my face; you can watch them in the weakening in my knees. Today I feel good. We're here on the beach. The sun is warm. Let's enjoy the moment. That's all we have."

We walked in silence for a while, matching our moods to the off-season, almost deserted shore. The thought crossed my mind that I could never create resources for others if I did not take time to refill my own reservoir. I realized, too, that women of my mother's generation pioneered the rights we of mine expect to receive. I said softly as the waves receded, "Thank you for enduring so much for the sake of my liberation." Mother wisely chose not to reply. Her inner strength and endurance offered me a living lesson worth sharing with others. To be a nurturing person is not only a physical but also a spiritual gift. "I pray for you from the minute your flight leaves the ground until you touch down." I, in turn, never underestimate the power of my parent's intercessory prayer nor her capacity for creativity.

I am reminded of a teacher of mine, long since retired, who worked on an assembly line in a factory during the war years. Like a broken record, she had to hear everyday about the inadequacy of the "weaker sex." Common sense told her to back off when she was asked to do something that might have endangered her life. Other ways could be found to prove the point that she was a skilled and competent worker. By steady productivity, by being where she was needed, she rose to a supervisory position long after more vocal protesters were dismissed. Once she became the boss of the electrical division, she set about improving conditions for all the workers.

Another woman I know chose to work quietly behind the scenes to foster the spiritual renewal of her parish despite the presence of an uncooperative pastor and parish council. She used methods of indirect rather than direct confrontation and communication. In the long run, the wisdom of moderation versus militancy prevailed. The parish now has one of the best adult leadership forums and formation programs in the diocese. She told me: "Women must prepare themselves to take and accept co-responsibility, but they must never lose their instinctive sense of when to step forward and when to hold back. Wise timing can make all the difference in regard to the success or failure of a good work."

We women need to pray daily for this sort of wisdom. It does not come automatically like water from a fountain. If anything, there are times when impulsiveness prevails, when stubbornness blocks the channels of creativity, when we react rather than respond to challenges and conflicts. We find ourselves ensnared in plans and projects that are not true to what we know needs to be done. We close our hearts and minds to God's voice. We forge ahead with our own agenda, only to fail miserably. There is no easy way to wisdom.

Wisdom also teaches us that our identity is not sourced solely in our work. Our worth is not invested in what we do but in the kind of woman we want to be. We must continue to fight for a just and peaceful world. God blesses our trying. It is up to us to overcome the urgency to set change in motion in accordance with our timetable, to be so fixated on instant results that we fail to hear the whispers of the infinite.

Self-love, pride, arrogance, and power are lauded as sound building blocks for success in an achievement-oriented world. But is this the way for Christian women? We run the risk of becoming efficient while losing any sense of edification. Haggard edges betray an unhappy heart. One look in the mirror can trigger the self-reflection that saves us from betraying the balance between contemplation and action.

Work is possible only if we are willing to rest in God. To be spiritual as well as functional caregivers, we must keep the channels of receptivity open and clear. By the same token, we know that good ideas remain only interior ideals unless we put them into practice.

> I think of Christ as being both wise and practical. His decision to include women among his disciples was wise. His having to name men among the twelve was practical. In both cases he changed the course of history, enabling women along with men to spread the gospel through a ministry of love and compassion and not by appointment only.

In fact, the silences about women in the scriptures may speak louder than words. Their presence in the life and ministry of Jesus must have been so obvious it was deemed unnecessary to record what everyone knew. Women taught, preached, opened their homes to the early community, and manifested extraordinary courage. They were martyred side by side with the men. Jesus' style of leadership seemed to draw forth a person's potential without focusing on his or her gender. His dispositions of openness and respect encouraged Peter to grow as much as Mary Magdalene.

Sociocultural pressures to conform may subtly coerce women to betray our inner convictions and gifts. Jesus calls us to remain courageous in the face of ridicule, to stand up for what we believe. One friend confesses that she has had to cope silently and verbally with many challenges to her decision to follow her call to full-time motherhood. She admits this commitment can be met because of her husband's cooperation, but she has also had to be outspoken in her conviction that homemaking is a noble calling in its own right. The secret to her peace of mind is the heartfelt conviction that faithfulness to one's call is an essential condition for self-fulfillment in Christ.

> My life flows more from the inside out rather than from the feeling of being pushed and prodded by outside pressures and

influences. Something would be missing like a black hole in space if I did not cultivate this sense of my personal worth. I put a lot of energy into developing significant relationships. I try to be honest with myself. Others tell me that I am one person with whom they can be themselves too. Some have said I have a special quality of peace about me. I do not see it, but I simply take them at their word. Letting others love me as I love them is a new twist. I'm trying to be as comfortable letting them care for me as I care for them.

Putting family needs first does not preclude finding a creative outlet for the expression of a woman's gifts in work outside the home. What matters is to maintain a sense of who one is in what one does. The wisdom of womanspirit is to listen in loving silence to our heart, to risk sharing what we hear with trusted others, and to give what we can of ourselves in response to everyday concerns. The point is: "Some degree of self-knowledge and self-acceptance is essential before we can really love and serve others."

What we know, but hesitate to admit, is that no effort, however noble, produces perfect results. Many are the times when we, as a family, plan to take the children to lunch or dinner, an event that begins with the obligatory lecture to behave well or never again.... Good manners last through the appetizer but by the time the entree is served, tensions are at a high point around the table. Soon the first glass of water spills and adults silently vow that this will be the last time we eat out until the children are teenagers! Expectations soar, actions seldom meet them. More often than not the most ordinary events turn into crisis situations. Does it take a brick wall to fall down before we face the fact that it is not in our power to reach perfection?

> It seems in my memory that each time I was totally devastated the problem was not conquered until I relented and turned it and my life once more wholly over to God. Abandonment is the answer. All things are possible only through God's grace.... through God's love re-energized in the Eucharist and seen and received from others. The more we demand perfection where none is possible, the less joy, love, and peace we experience. God will give us all we need if only we have the humility to ask.

As one on whom many others lean, a woman needs to remember that she is a person with gifts and talents as well as limitations and faults. She is free and equal before God, but she must stand her ground, state her terms, give and receive love generously, and forgive quickly. As a Christian, she will come to see as the years pass by, with their delights and disappointments, that life without a personal love relationship with the Trinity is no life at all. Whatever we do, wherever we go, we are all in need of a Savior who cares for us intimately.

Life can be tender or tough, challenging or complacent. Our eternal destiny does not come upon us during some distant tomorrow; it is with us now. We cannot endure this mystery of fallibility alone. We need the companionship of Christ to carry us through the times when we long to be made whole. Either we stand with Christ at our side or we become an entity unto ourselves.

Women today may unwittingly choose this kind of autonomy, this false sense of total independence or self-sufficiency, even if it means the right to sever the life in their womb. To reach such a conclusion suggests that a woman has not learned the lesson of clinging like a child in the dark to the hand of God. God's nearness, especially when it is our turn to carry the cross, is the barometer against which we can gauge our actions and decisions, our sense of right or wrong, our option for what is life-giving and our rejection of what is life-denying. As one woman told me:

> I now approve of myself because I know I am approved of by God in whose form and likeness I am wonderfully, fearfully made. I know that God has granted me the freedom to choose life and to bring what is fully alive physically and spiritually into this world. All knowing and utterly faithful is God's concern for you and me. That is why it is impossible to keep our gracious acts as well as our mistakes from God's sight. The divine will is that we recover our own gift of insight, that we learn by trial and error to enjoy every moment of life, and that we strive to relate to one another in gratitude for our gifts. Where there is discord in our hearts or in our relationships, we must strive to draw God into the picture and find a way to repair what is broken before it is too late.

The first person rage harms is the one who harbors it in her heart. Women must be persons who choose peace, who oppose war in any form. We must preach and practice reverence for every facet of God's creation from streams in backyard woods to stars in the Milky Way. We women can change the world. With God's help we can find a way to move away from divisions that destroy the possibility of peace. We are even now on the verge of binding things great and small to the loving heart of God.

Allow me to share at the close of this chapter excerpts from letters written by women to daughters, friends, co-workers, and community members, with whom it is worth sharing a little wisdom gained from living. This one is from a mother to her youngest daughter, a sophomore in college:

Dear Sandra:

In response to your question about selecting a major, all I can say is, look deeply into your heart and ask yourself, "Are my personal goals centered on having a good time, on career objectives, or on my worth as a person in God's eyes? Do I want to be swayed by the push and pull of materialism or by the inner voice of the Spirit?

At this time of your life you are still actively forming your identity, who you are as a woman before God. Are you self-affirming and helpful to others? I know that what you are learning places emphasis on rational decision making, but don't forget to listen with the ears of your heart. Material and intellectual production are high on the Western scale of values, but there is more to life than mere consumption.

I know that it seems as if those who take are more powerful than those who give. But don't be fooled by surface success. Transformation is not a matter of manipulating life by virtue of the will. It requires a delicate touch to respond to graces already given. First be open to receive, then do all you can to serve what is good and holy.

Be a person committed to calling attention to the truth. Fight for what you believe, for justice and peace, but cushion your concerns in prayer and reflection lest you risk becoming overly strident or dismayed. Change will happen, also in regard to women's concerns, but not overnight.

Let your desire for integration override the need to analyze everything to death. Try to be true to your feelings and less judgmental of yourself and others. Balance your need for intimacy with your awareness of how much more an enduring commitment will meet it.

My advice would be not to spend too much energy on seeking that special "one and only" for the time being. If something happens, cross that bridge, but don't push against the pace of grace. That kind of love will come in God's good time.

Above all, don't knuckle under to peer pressure or allow anyone to undermine your sense of what is right and wrong. What you are learning and with whom you associate will influence your lifestyle in a lasting way.

Pray fervently for help and trust that I will be praying with and for you. Treasure your sense of the poetic, the aesthetic, the mystical, and don't stop dreaming your dreams. The challenge is to keep them alive with candor and courage.

When I was your age, I received a letter similar to this one from your grandmother. Listen to what she said to me several years ago:

> "It is as wonderful to be a woman as it is to wake up in the morning. Our femininity is a special gift. How you think, feel, react, and act affects everyone around you. When you find your purpose for existence, you will come closest to touching the face of God, to being and becoming free . . . "

So, dear, treasure every experience of sight, sound, touch, taste, and smell God gives you. Share these moments with someone you love, for they are God's gifts to you. Marvel at your capacity as a woman to be a lifegiver in and with God.

There will be easy times in the years to come and many difficult ones. Enjoy and endure them all. I hope you will be able to accept what comes from the hand of God, who has loved you from the start and who has called you "favored."

Your grandmother's words taught me that human love is a greater gift than gold. When all else fails, God's love is everlasting. In your darkest days, remember how acceptable you are in God's eyes. Knit this conviction into the fabric of your life: You are loved, my dear, you are loved!

As ever, Mother

This next letter comes from a young woman, writing to her friend, a man she has known since college days. Both are pursuing their careers in different areas of the country, but they try to maintain regular correspondence. Recently they have been reflecting on their friendship in relation to their professional life.

Dear Steven:

I would have to say that one of the best parts of our togetherness is the appreciation we feel for one another's gifts. We are alike in many ways, but we also are free to celebrate our differences. Our thought patterns, our mind sets, move in unique directions, but we share in the search for answers to the same questions.

I am touched by your gentleness — as when you admit that you have hurt me, and feel sorry — and I know that with you I do not have to hide my strength.

The problem arises for both of us when we act within the context of our professional roles. We become so intensely involved with what we are doing that we have difficulty shifting the priority to our relationship.

I admit that roles can become figural in my life, but in my finer moments I know how much more I value our friendship. It takes priority over any of my functional plans and projects.

Does this tension between being and doing have to do with my/our interest in integration? In relational issues? I hope our roles will not get in the way of further reflection. If we start to compete with one another, even subtly, we will despoil the cohesiveness that makes what we have so special.

When we really talk — about our frustrations with work and family relations, about the conflicts that ensue because of career choices, about our faithfulness or lack of it to God's call — we end up having the best time. The conversation flows and we realize how counterproductive it is to underestimate our importance to one another.

Respect is the glue that cements our relationship. I have a strong sense of our being equal in dignity in God's eyes. A woman in my office shared with me a horrible experience of the opposite. Her husband of twenty-five years made love to her passionately the night before he told her he wanted a divorce because he's in love with another woman. How a woman recovers from such a blow is beyond me. Men who see sex as an isolated act outside of a committed relationship will never be able to understand a woman's feelings about fidelity.

As friends we enjoy mutuality, but we would be nowhere without trust and respect. You are other than me, I am other than you, yet there is a oneness between us, an ability to communicate in serious and humorous ways that is unique. God's gifts to you have been given to me and mine have become yours. This sharing is surely the best feature of our friendship. We truly care for one another and for that gift thanks is too small a word.

Love, as ever, Jenny

This is a letter written by a religious educator to one of her co-workers. It deals with relations between professional women striving to express Christian excellence in the workplace.

Dear Terry:

I want to tell you again that I could not have survived this week were it not for the sense that we are together in a task that transcends all of us.

The project to which we are committed has enabled us to go beyond personality differences and find common ways to pursue our goals. I am happy we can be so honest with one another. None of us would want to spend hours trying to analyze our somewhat irascible temperaments.

What I value most about you and the other women in our office is our ability to see not only the particulars of this or any project, but the whole picture — not only the disparate parts but how they blend and work together.

It is my conviction that women learn from childhood to see in terms of the "whole" and to serve its unfolding. In our work we must offer hospitality to strangers, teach God's word, nurture and attend to needs.

The ways in which we women relate to one another, to others, and to God are only now being appreciated and promoted. I am glad we make a point of encouraging this desire to define and celebrate our gifts.

We sense being on a journey to a new era in the church. We acknowledge and draw upon what each person has to offer. When we come together as colleagues, when we express confidence in one another, a new-found energy is released. The sharing of our story as women in the church is a source of inspiration. When one of us is silent, another speaks. Issues are brought to the fore, and we work to resolve them, even if it means agreeing to disagree agreeably!

I remember a nurse I came to know through a series of hospitalizations. She had the uncanny gift of caring from the heart. Her methods were old-fashioned but effective: hugs, hand stroking, eye contact, looking at and listening to you, touching. We patients could not wait for her to enter our rooms.

When women lose this capacity to care, they lose their effectiveness as channels through which divine love flows into a wounded world. This nurse did not need a multiplicity of words. Her presence had the proper effect — sick people felt better when she walked through the door.

Sometimes I think we women use too many words trying to justify our experience. Silence can be an appropriate response, too, especially in the face of persecution.

There are a lot of forums created by feminist thinkers to air controversial views. These are good. But there are also times when words must cease, when action has to become contemplative.

When we as friends and co-workers have the courage to dismantle the defenses and simply be present to one another, we can unite for a common purpose and enjoy together the completion of a project — of no worth to any of us unless it is pleasing to God. You know that without your support none of this would be possible. See you at next week's planning meeting.

God bless you, as ever, Betty

Finally, I want to share this copy of a yearly letter sent by a sister I know to members of her community and a few other lay friends.

Dear Sisters:

This salutation is special. It signifies the closeness and understanding we feel. By contrast, I remember an incident that occurred when I was in college. I found out that a girl-friend had broken our movie date because she had gotten a real date with a boy and I was only a "woman friend." I was in her eyes dispensable. That memory still upsets me.

I wonder if we really know how important it is as women to honor one another in our womanliness.

Recently I went to a get-together of professional women. It was a wonderful weekend. Newcomers to the group spoke openly about the challenges they were facing in the marketplace. We reached levels of helpfulness seldom attained in our isolated offices. Even bitter feelings toward issues like sexual harassment in the workplace began to dissipate in the knowledge that woman-to-woman support is a great deterrent to domineering or condescending behavior.

This decision to connect rather than to become conflictual was more rewarding than trying to fit ourselves as women into a harness of projects or expectations alien to our creativity.

Women admitted that it was tempting to accept a competitive viewpoint as the only standard of success in our culture. It is only in recent times that we have begun to realize the value and viability of women's scholarship and the feminine perspective on history, literature, and theology.

I am learning, Dear Sisters, to see the good and humorous side of all these situations, to let go of my neatly defined timetables, and to remain calm and patient in the face of cataclysmic change.

Most of all, I am trying to place my trust in God. In imitation of Christ, I strive to remain sensitive to both the material and spiritual needs of the poor. I confess praying as I've never prayed previously. Even in the darkest nights I am confident the Spirit is with us, leading us to a new era of equality and respect.

I am becoming more detached about things that used to deafen my ears to God's voice. I worry less and wonder more. Some say I'm less irritable, definitely less driven. I feel as if I am becoming freer, more accepting of suffering, more compassionate about the broken bits that comprise our human condition.

The vision of women binding wounds was vivid one day in my Bible study group. I suddenly ceased listening to the ladies' voices and only looked, as if through a soft mist, at their faces. I felt a surge of love shoot through me. Gathered in that room was a friend recently diagnosed with a degenerative disease and, by her own admission, soon to be bed-ridden. Another member, severely diabetic, was still caring for elderly parents along with her husband and children. One suffered frightening bouts with depression and had been in and out of therapy until taking a sudden turn for the better six months ago — about the time our group began. Still another was facing a financial crunch because her pension plan had not produced the expected yield. The last had lost her husband, the father of their three children, to a massive heart attack two years ago.

These women are jewels in the crown of God. They are brave, faithful souls, wanting to read and absorb the living word of God. What an example they are, collectively and alone, of sorrow and grace, of courage and joy. How good it is to be together in this small Christian community, uplifted by the love that pervades this room. Its power lessens our personal pain and gives us the strength to find in every end a new beginning.

There is much quiet bravery among God's people. It would be tempting for women to sink away in self-pity and anger. Instead we choose to rise with the sun to a new day's dawning. We may be wounded, but we are not withered. If anything, the opposite is true. We seek new ways of expressing our womanhood. We experience what it means to give of ourselves to God and others in the present moment. It is as necessary to let go of the past as it is not to dwell too anxiously on the future.

These words from the Book of Wisdom were our closing prayer that day. Accept them as my gift to you. Have a blessed New Year.

Sister Paula

> . . . she is an aura of the might of God
>   and a pure effusion of the glory of the Almighty:
>   therefore nought that is sullied enters into her.
>
> For she is the refulgence of eternal light,
>   the spotless mirror of the power of God
>   the image of [God's] goodness.

And she, who is one, can do all things,
    and renews everything while herself perduring.

And passing into holy souls from age to age,
    she produces friends of God and prophets.

For there is nought God loves, be it not one
    who dwells with Wisdom.

For she is fairer than the sun
    and surpasses every constellation of the stars.

Compared to light, she takes precedence;
    for that, indeed, night supplants,
    but wickedness prevails not over Wisdom.

                    (Ws. 7:26–39)

> *It is when things go wrong, when*
> *the good things do not happen, when*
> *our prayers seem to have been lost,*
> *that God is most present. We do*
> *not need the sheltering wings when*
> *things go smoothly. We are closest*
> *to God in the darkness, stumbling*
> *along blindly.*
> — *Madeleine L'Engle*

Winters in a Woman's Life

*F*ROM WHAT I KNOW OF MYSELF, it would be impossible to live in a city where I could not enjoy the change of seasons. I am a Northeasterner by birth. The geographic and climatic conditions in this part of the country suit my temperament and match my moods. Since building my own home in 1985 on a wooded plot several miles from the downtown area, I have had the chance to observe the rhythms of nature in a way I could not do when I was living in an apartment.

Dividing the dining from the living room is a cathedral window out of which I can see ridge upon ridge of the rolling hills of western Pennsylvania. A side road in eye's view snakes from the bottom of the hill westward toward the airport. It is a better forecaster of the weather than the radio announcer. Out of my window, I can watch a row of trees, some of which I planted, yield to nature's moodswings. I can stand rapt by the power of a pending storm or catch the glow of a moonbeam on dewy grass.

Into my window surges spring. I watch the wild abandonment of robins on the wing, fluttering hither and yon in search of straw and weeds to build their nests beneath the rafters of my front deck. As tulips and daffodils poke through partially frozen flower plots, I feel winter's torpor departing. It is as if my own shivering appendages no longer need to hold tight to themselves to keep warm. Cold fingers and toes can stretch toward the faint yet glowing rays of sun that will soon tease the crocuses into bloom. Before long it will be time to rake the leftover leaves, thatch the lawn, clean out the bird feeder, and turn over the soil in my flower boxes. Spring means that Easter is near and with it the joy of the resurrection, the promise of new life, ever to be renewed.

Summer in our section of the country is a lush and lazy time of year. Out of my window on the world, I watch hazy heat rise from the asphalt. Inside I hear the air conditioner click on. Fat robins feed on worms that slither across the blacktop after late afternoon thunderstorms. The bushes near the driveway almost overnight burst fully into bloom. The weeds in the flower boxes grow in a frenzy of fertility that forces me to pick and pull, prune and seed, after work hours and on weekends to keep the yard from becoming a rain forest in the city.

Summer is as fruitful a time for creativity as it is for farm market produce. It is when I do most of my writing and lecture preparation. This is the season that grants me the luxury of blocks of time. With pen and paper in hand, I like to sit on my shady deck and see what happens. Sometimes the words are as sparse as drops from a faucet. At other times they flash as fast as fire that flames charcoal for outdoor cooking.

I love the way the sun warms my body early in the morning when I most want and need to write. There is an urgency in the words then, as if they cannot wait to appear on paper. The steaming coffee, the rising sun, the sounds of summer, the flow of symbols coalesce in splendid creativity. Though I am sitting on the deck in a redwood chair, it feels as if I am riding in a raft over white water on a hot July afternoon. I have nothing to do but strap on my life jacket, relax, and flow with the river's rough and tumble play. Any effort to steer the raft is useless if it conflicts with the water's rush from the gorge to the shallows. At such moments, admittedly rare, writing is not work. It is pure gift. Words roll over one another like snapping turtles cracking through their shells and slipping into the sea. One sentence gives birth to the next in a generativity of images and symbols that a writer does not control but serves. One becomes a medium of the message as surely as song birds announce at dawn's brink that summer is near.

Soon enough the cathedral window frames leaves turning from red to gold to brown. September announces another season in nature and in daily life. It signifies that it is time to reenter the workforce. Instead of obeying the call of birds, I must listen to the pencil marks on my pocket calendar, replete with appointments that had to be kept "yesterday." A month ago I could languish in bed, relishing the feel of pre-dawn breezes on my face. Now I have to bound out from under warm covers if I want to get a head-start on the day. The fall air is cool, crisp, conducive to fostering competence. I feel a surge of energy, electric, like crackling leaves underfoot. Projects started in the summer come to fruition. I find myself working overtime, developing research projects, packing for speaking engagements, finalizing program planning. It would be easy to lose my center if I forgot to look out the window into a world awash with earthy hues — the colors I favor in my decor: burnt amber and moonlit gold, orange squash and chestnut brown. My mood is one of anticipation as when a child waits for the last leaf to fall. Thanksgiving comes and goes. Wild geese migrate over-head. The hum of locust wings ceases as if forecasting the hush of winter.

One morning I awaken, brew coffee, and amble to the win-dow. I raise the shade and see snow obscuring all that had been brown or green. Mixed with freezing rain, the combination makes my driveway a sheet of ice. It is the season when seeds go under-ground to die with no visible sign that new life is stirring within. Winter symbolizes a time of hardship, when we suffer for the sake of growing wise. The whiteness of the snow outside my window reminds me of blank paper on which a story has to be written. There are many winters in a woman's life. An elderly friend of mine still remembers this one with fear:

She is only five years old. Because times are tough during the Great Depression, her parents need to take in boarders to make some extra money. Mostly her mother is at home, but today she has to go shopping. The little girl is left in the care of her older sister, who goes over to a neighbor's yard while she naps. She awakens to find the boarder by her bedside running his thumb softly up and down her cheek. He says he will take her to the bathroom when she starts to whimper. She draws back, but he tells her everything is fine, not to be afraid. Talking softly and touching her, he unbuttons her pants and sets her on the commode. Then, standing over her, he unzippers his trousers and tells her he has something special for her to see and hold in her hand. She remembers jumping off the seat and slipping at top speed between his legs, for he was over six feet tall. She runs for her life into her parents' room and hides like a scared rabbit under the bed, a four-poster backed tight against the wall. She cowers in the farthest corner shaking from head to foot, terrified that "it" might reach in and grab her. The boarder paces around the open sides of the bed, calling her crude names, then soft, cooing endearments. She does not budge. She feels the bed moving above her. She hears her heart beat as fast as a frightened bird's. Her only thought is, "Mama, help me," and, like a miracle, she appears, beating the beast with a broomstick and chasing him out of the house. She is safe, but the memory of this close call with a child molester never leaves her. It is winter in a little girl's life.

Winter is a time when women sometimes feel the pieces of their life, so carefully welded together, beginning to split apart like icy cracks in a once solidly frozen pond. I experienced such a winter moment in my life when, after much prayer and appraisal, I decided to resign from a tenured university teaching position to devote myself fulltime to the ministry of lay formation.

I am going through an inner winter of detachment, even though my new work commences in July. I have truly given my all to academic and administrative life for the past twenty-one years. Now, led by grace and good spiritual guidance, I am preparing to serve as the executive director of a growing ecumenical association established as a center of research, resource development, and publication. Packing and moving boxes of books and papers from the campus to my office feels like pulling tacks out of a wall to which they have been stuck for as long as one can remember. To "de-tack" is the literal meaning of detachment. I can testify from experience how wrenching the movement from one way of life to another can be. When relational bonds break like links in a weakened chain, when new friendships have to be formed, it is winter in a woman's life.

A few years after my father's death, after months of indecisiveness, my mother found a buyer for our family home and an apartment she liked. Time seems to stand still. The pain of packing a lifetime's worth of personal treasures into paper cartons is in her eyes. Some she will keep, most will be sent to the Salvation Army or the St. Vincent de Paul Society. I take photos of the emptying of each room. Emotions collide as she says her good-byes to the house she helped to build, to her beloved home.

I remember the misty May morning moving trucks pull into the driveway. Though it is early spring, winter wraps around the empty house and around my mother's heart. Unable to watch a whole life being loaded by the movers, we get into my car and go to a neighborhood café for breakfast. It is about 7:30 in the morning. Dew covers newly cut lawns. The weekend streets are relatively free of traffic. The air is still. We feel suspended between two time zones. On the way to eat, driving down a steep hill, we slow to a snail's pace, not knowing what to say. The emotions between us run too deep for words. Suddenly the silence is shattered by a simultaneous gasp of astonishment. There on the hillside in the middle of the city are two deer grazing, a fawn and a doe. I cut the engine and we glide quietly to the side of the road, watching the animals in awed silence. They look like statues poised in attention. Our eyes meet, then, in a flash, they leap across the road and into the woods. Their appearance is pure gift. It shakes loose the sadness that has strained our speech. We laugh and dub them our good luck charm, nature's confirmation of a move that would prove in the end to be as liberating for her as for the rest of the family.

These paradoxical winter-into-spring moments in a woman's life parallel shifts in the seasons. Where I live March can never seem to decide whether to move toward spring bonnets or hold tenaciously to winter blasts. It is hard to tell whether crises spell danger or opportunity or a mix of both. Once in the midst of summer I felt the hand of winter gripping my heart with no apparent promise of spring.

I am living in an apartment overlooking the city. It offers a dramatic view of the three rivers, the Renaissance skyline, and the entire urban campus to which I commute for work every day. Recently the institute has been rehoused in the Administration Building, the tallest, most visible structure on the Bluff. I stand in front of my triangular picture window watching a violent summer storm blowing down the Monongahela, heading east. The clouds are ominous, the lightning quick zig-zag slashes of white light, full of fire. Then the worst happens. I watch in disbelief as a bolt touches down directly atop the building that contains every scrap of our operation — current and archival files, student records, audio-visual equipment. The list of what we could live without, what it would be devastating to lose, leaps into my mind as I bound down the stairs and into my car.

I watch as smoke, then flames rise from the roof. I am on site as the fire engines, police cars, and ambulances arrive. Distraught faculty like myself and curious onlookers gather to await the worse.

Luckily it is a holiday weekend. The few people in the building are safely evacuated. I pray that the fire will be contained before it breaks through the third floor ceiling and into our offices. We learn several hours later that the actual fire is out but that the water damage to our department is severe.

University officials offer me the choice between a few dormitory rooms or four large classrooms on the top of a building without elevators in which to reassemble what is left of our damaged and undamaged property. I agree to the classroom offer even while the immensity of the work ahead of me momentarily paralyzes my initiative. Who will help me reassemble an entire department, carry hundreds of boxes, filthy furniture, and soggy books and files up four flights of stairs?

None of our own students are around. I am the only responsible administrator in charge. Our director is in Holland. The dangerous aspect of crisis looms perilously close. It feels as if I am walking on an icy sidewalk with spike-heeled pumps. There is no time to lose. Something has to be done and quickly! By Tuesday morning I have recruited undergraduates from several summer classes to carry at least one box each up the four flights. I need everyone from the basketball team to the janitorial staff to help me turn disaster into a new direction. I lose count of the time it takes to scrub charred desks, clean artifacts, and rearrange open classrooms into office cubicles. Following countless hours of hard work and prayer, we are ready to open our doors to the Fall '75 class.

I, as many women, have had experiences that start badly and end up being transforming. Adversity sparks aspiration. Not the coldest wind could deter my father from drilling through solid ice to fish for one last catch. We children caught the spirit of confidence in crisis from him. A woman in our neighborhood with crippling arthritis walks three miles a day simply to keep moving. Another, rather than caring for her aging parents alone, has started an elder day care center. A bright intelligent social worker I know had a near fatal automobile accident that left her severely brain damaged, yet for three years she has struggled to recover her speaking ability and has even attained employment in the postal service.

These tales of brokenness and recovery reveal that winters in a woman's life are also wellsprings of hope. Moments of deeper awareness of one's life direction may be subtle as well as traumatic.

The forming mystery can be as delicate as the brush of a feather, as dramatic as the rage of a coastal storm.

She is about thirty-five, unmarried, good-looking, a flight attendant. She walks into the airport bathroom where I am combing my hair and exchanges glances with a woman about three years younger than she, who is nursing her infant son. The eyes of the two women meet. The mother smiles. The stewardess remarks how adorable the child is, a real sweetheart. I begin to wonder if at this moment she is secretly questioning her life of constant travel but no commitments, of fun but no family to call her own and keep her company. Who does she see every time she glances in the mirror? Is this brief encounter a winter moment in her life?

When I accompanied a friend to Mayo Clinic several years ago, I met another "woman in waiting," a mother from Romania whose child had a genetic heart defect that required corrective surgery. She and I sat together in the family room for what was truly a winter's night of cold uncertainty. She told me of the exceptional courage the child showed for a boy of seven. He never complained. It was only through the grace of God that they had gathered the funds to come to the clinic. Her strong faith restored my spirit. I had come to the cliff's edge of anxiety over my friend's condition. Her confidence in God, her courage as a mother, helped me through the worst hours of waiting. As day passed into night, the patients for whom we were praying moved from critical to stable condition. We embraced each other in joy and thanksgiving. We felt as if mercy divine had touched all of us with tender, healing care. Were it only true that every story ended so happily.

It was again mid-summer on the yearly calendar, deep winter on the roster of experience. I am conducting a week-long workshop on the theme of living the spiritual disciplines. On the day in question I present material on the dispositions of openness and awe in relation to the exercises of silence and formative reading. A knock on the door interrupts our question-and-answer period. The secretary of the department has a message for one of the students. He asks permission to leave and that is the last I see of him. The next day word comes from the chairperson that sends a shock wave through the class. A counselor had to break the news to this student that his twenty-year-old son had been killed in a head-on collision with a drunken driver. We mourn for his loss at an ecumenical service. Sitting in the chapel, I wonder privately, in the face of such injustice, what the words we had shared in class about gentleness and forgiveness would mean now? Would I know what to say to him about nonjudgmentalism if he knocked on my office door today? It was as if arctic icebergs had floated into Anaheim where they lived. It would be months before the boy's mother and father felt any diminishment of grief, a lifetime, and then some, to recover from such a loss.

For the remainder of the workshop, this family's tragedy was evidence enough that life does hang by a gossamer thread. Finitude is the frozen tundra we all must cross. Women, perhaps more so than men, are willing to share the winters of their life with one another. Private depressions are alleviated by open discussions. Partings from family members, friends, lovers, and co-workers leave empty spaces only new loves and more trustworthy relations can fill. Women have told me that winters often commence when they have not felt understood.

Because it is late at night and all but a few of us are sleeping, I cannot help but overhear the couple behind me on the bus quibbling. She accuses him of never listening; he responds by saying she has become a real drag. She says he never spends time with her, except on brief vacations; he retaliates by asking her if she has a clue about how hard he works. That is not the point . . . their cutting words bounce back and forth from court to court as if they are competing for points in a tennis match. Neither understands the other, that is clear; yet both are desperate to achieve some semblance of communication and communion. The coolness of the February night air matches this couple's stand-off attitude. They live side by side in constant conflict, probably lonelier now than when they were single. To think one's dream has come true, only to find one's world falling apart, is the worst of winters in a woman's life.

A similar sense of isolation overtakes the young woman placed by her peers on a pedestal. She postures the allure of aloofness, when underneath the mask of self-sufficiency, she is as shy as a snowbird. Labeled stuck-up, she chooses a table for one, when in reality all she seeks is relief from her solitude. Older women may experience winter at the midpoint of life, around the time of menopause, or when a relationship that began on a romantic high flattens like a bottle of uncapped soda. Depending on who she is, a woman may watch soap operas and wonder if she should shake loose of sanctions, have an affair, start a second career, or get a face lift. When life falls to pieces, people risk losing sight of the larger picture. The same happens to men at midlife, to be sure, but women seem to sense the passing of youthful expectations and physical stamina with special poignancy.

I remember as a child dreading to hear my father's solemn announcement when it was time to go home after a day of fun and good food: "The picnic is over." Endings might signify new beginnings, but this does not diminish their sting. The French believe that to depart is to die a little. When a spouse dies, as my mother knows, the widow or widower may only slowly recover from the loss. Time heals, but not at once. A child sits and weeps on the empty veranda where "Daddy" used to sit. An unused mug is the one from which "Mommy" drank coffee every morning. His or her closet is stale from being unopened. Tools collect cobwebs in the garage and the sewing machine remains rusted and unopened. Tears enough fall to form a river of winters. Many people pray solely for the courage to carry on.

I feel this way when I awaken on cold, snowy mornings, aware after one peek out the window that I have to bundle up and head for the bus. The driveway of my house slopes steeply from the front terrace to the road. It is impassable for several weeks. My only access route is a narrowly shoveled path from the back door through my brother's yard to the main street. The winter seems interminably prolonged on mornings such as these. All I want to do is hibernate in the warmth of my bed until the first sign of spring. Yet, the truth is, this season is like a tunnel. The only way out is the way through.

There are times in a woman's life when winter never seems to end. She is involved in an abusive relationship and cannot muster the courage to seek counseling. She has been betrayed by a trusted friend and cannot foresee any hope of reconciliation. She is in a hospital waiting room when the surgeon matter-of-factly announces that her husband of five years has, at most, only a few months left to live. Her baby dies at birth and for months thereafter she cannot overcome her depression.

Such times seem devoid of hope, without redemption. One's heart seems cracked as ice, muddy as melting snow. What used to be clear is shadowed by clouds of ambiguity. Neither faith nor family can supply ready answers to such an abyss of loss and disappointment. Prayers appear to be unanswered, words clink like frozen cubes in an empty glass. The world is without why, and winter darkness holds back the light.

Yet signs of life somehow start to appear. Falling snow becomes falling rain. Sunlight sparkles on the last mounds of frozen slush, sending shafts of white light through the window, enough to warm the living room, if I do not open the door.

Affliction hastens the flight from winter to spring as we witness in the lives of brave women like Anne Frank, Etty Hillesum, Edith Stein, and Flannery O'Connor. Though their way was blocked by imprisonment, physical debilitation, misunderstanding, and a host of other ills, they were led to a liberation of spirit few attain. These women, all of whom died young, were entrapped in winters of persecution, but none lost their sense of inner peace. Their journals, letters, essays, and narratives reveal that all grew in courage and in the comprehension of human tragedy. Their voices consoled others crushed by sorrow and helped them to regain joy. Anne Frank's conviction that people were good at heart, though cruelty held her in captivity and Etty Hillesum's postcard flung from the train transporting her to certain death, assuring her friends that she and the other inmates of the prison camp had left the depot singing for joy, are two out of thousands of examples of the death-to-life, defeat-to-return, winter-to-spring paradoxes women know so well from experience.

Nothing can deter women of faith from breaking through ice floes of despair and rekindling hope. My sense is that women who have not wrestled with the dragon of doubt, who have not faced winters of discontent, risk remaining superficial, unspirited persons, lacking depth and wisdom. Each woman whose story has been imprinted on my heart has grown slowly and painfully to spiritual maturity. None would have wanted to escape the crucible in which God's grace turned their dross into gold.

My driveway is the best barometer signaling when a shift of season is about to occur. Melting snow flows in long rivulets down the edges of the asphalt to the street. Warmed by the sun, the blacktop surface reappears. Muddy mounds melt down. The crush of ice begins to crack. Shoveling becomes less a dreaded chore, more a sign of success, because at last I can see the results of my efforts. However long the stretch of winter is, it cannot hold back the thrust of spring. Who of us does not know a family where a handicapped child has become the catalyst for communion between formerly selfish siblings? A dysfunctional couple with a history of substance abuse finally cuts the chain of repeated betrayals by seeking counseling. A wife, early widowed, goes back to work and successfully raises six children.

These reversals are the substance of womanspirit, accounting for the grace of perseverance amidst pain, creativity amidst chaos, restoration after woundedness. The more one survives such challenges, the stronger one grows as a woman or man of faith. In their crosses, women and men of courage see signs of God's glory. "What makes the desert beautiful," says Antoine de Saint Exupery, "is that somewhere, deep inside it, there is a spring." When and how does this inner transformation occur? To chart its course is as impossible as trying to detect what dynamics nature has set in motion beneath the snow. How does our human spirit come in tune with the Holy Spirit? How does winter know when to give way to spring? The answers to such questions never emerge with crystalline clarity. The word comes into our heart as soft as newfallen snow, in whispers encouraging us to step aside and start again, not to give up; in invitations to put the past to rest and live in the present; in challenges to drop stale, no longer viable, ways of relating and seek new friendships; in appeals to respond to others more openly, with trust and patience freed of expectations of personal gain.

Our spirit is as resilient as rose bushes after an early frost. It revives like bones uncreaking after ice-bound mornings when we promise anew to seek God's will in the simplicity of the present moment. We must forget the past with its burden of failure and guilt, if we want to feel the lightness of spring.

Winter changes course so often that to survive requires wise planning. One never knows quite when the weather will take a turn for the worse nor when the forecasters will be wrong. One has to deal with any eventuality from jump-starting a dead battery to reheating frozen water pipes. To escape the doldrums of long dark days and nights would be a dream come true. Instead we may have to content ourselves with just noticeable improvements. What the future holds may not be as wild and wonderful as we might like but at least the weight of the cross we have been carrying may lighten a little as we turn it over to Christ, whose friendship never falters.

Winter tests, spring renews, our spirit. Dark hours endured in trust and faith teach us to appreciate what is lasting in this passing world. God's love for us is total and tender, as overwhelming as a winter blast, as gentle as a soft spring breeze. Along life's way, we meet as many messengers of divine mercy as there are stars in the sky on a clear cold night. There is wonder everywhere if we take time to behold the beauty that surrounds us as well as to explore the vast continent within.

Once my nephew told me he was thinking so hard about how he was put together that he banged his head into a locker door. That's a perfect description of the awe disposition. Stunned as we may be by what is happening to us, we can still stay open to good news when it announces itself. After all, we celebrate the birth of Christ in the middle of a season associated with frozen wastelands unsupportive of most forms of life. This is the season when Christ takes on our form in all things but sin. Winter is an epiphany of redemption, when death itself loses its sting.

Light fills the sky on this night of nights. The chill in the air cannot quell the warm feeling birth brings. The promised One, the Word of God becomes flesh and dwells among us to teach the nations what it means to live in peace and good will. Sufferers in Christ's name become ambassadors of compassion. Lonely persons become companions within a community of caring others.

On the night before Christmas eve, a few years ago, a dear friend of mine died of a heart attack while dining at a neighborhood restaurant. Family, friends, colleagues, even students who hardly knew him, were stunned by the suddenness of his demise. As a professor of philosophy, he had had to respond to the mystery of being and nonbeing. As a committed Christian, he had often expressed his belief in "the resurrection and the life." Neither the memory of his gifts as a teacher nor the depth of his faith could comfort us now. Despite the lights twinkling on a thousand trees, Christmas had lost its splendor. The season of birth was once again a season of death. What should have been a time of rejoicing became a time of mourning.

A month earlier, during what was to be our last visit, my friend had been his witty, reflective self. After a long conversation, he confirmed and blessed my decision to devote myself on a full-time basis to the ministry of lay formation while continuing to teach part-time as a visiting professor. He had made an extremely generous donation to our association and, as we learned later, named us in his will. On the day of his burial, it was so cold breathing was painful. Wind gusts whipped snow drifts over the cemetery roads.

The rest of the winter seemed to match that day. False thaws were followed by sudden vicious freezes. The weeks dragged toward spring with the speed of a wing weighed down by frozen water. As the seasons turned, the goodness and beauty of his spirit became more apparent. In his letters and poems, in his many books, who he was as a scholar and a Christian became inseparable from one another. He would have seen nothing heroic in his life, nothing particularly inspiring about the convicted passion of his faith. His customary gestures of self-effacement, his ready wit, hid his powers of reflection, the clarity of his mind, on matters of ultimate concern.

Another friend and I had driven to the airport a few days before Thanksgiving for a flight to Baltimore on what was to be our final visit with him. The departure schedule read "Cancelled" because of a furious winter storm that had left roads in the area snow covered and treacherous. I felt so compelled to carry on that we returned to the car and drove there. That evening we were able to talk and laugh together as if we had not a care in the world.

I want to stress how essential it is for women and men to trust their spirit at such moments. Logic told me to go home and hibernate until the storm passed; intuition said, "Forget the forecast and press on." One can smile condescendingly about this "wisdom of the heart," but without it women would not get through winters worse than this. When the voice within speaks, it is wise to listen. When an inner prompting leads us one way rather than another, following the first thought is often the best course of action. When in the gloom of night, we are able to set our sights on the light, there is no reason to doubt the cessation of winter. One look out the window reveals the coming of a new season when death will have turned into life as surely as twigs on brown trees bud green and birdsong breaks into windows thrown open to warmer winds.

Be careful; do not listen to the voice of your natural reasoning. You can expect just such reasoning to well up within you. Nonetheless, you must believe that you can abandon yourself utterly to the Lord for all your lifetime and that he will give you the grace to remain there! You must trust in God, "hoping against hope." (Romans 4:18)

— *Madame Guyon*

Wellsprings of Hope
in a Wounded World

*T*HERE ARE TIMES when I wish I did not feel as deeply as I do about small digs and subtle putdowns, about past hurts that threaten the hope of restored relations, about superficial chatter that passes for solid conversation. I would like my penchant for reflection to pause as easily as I can stop the action on my home video. I want to reel in my heart's emotions, to slow down the rush from winter to spring. And yet, as favorite authors like Anne Morrow Lindbergh and Annie Dillard would agree, without experiences of intense passion, there would be no hope of composition. Creativity requires the disruption of complacency. Words wrenched from deep furrows of feeling affect the unfolding of a woman's life.

"Paper is patient," wrote Anne Frank in her *Diary of a Young Girl*. Had her life followed the ordinary course, she might have found nothing worthy of recording. Anne's emotions ranged the gamut from girlish crushes to the gross anticipation of death in a concentration camp. Enforced solitude became the site of her spiritual release. Involuntary incarceration in a tiny attic with terrified adults for whom survival was the only issue and with a shy boy for whom lasting love was an impossibility transformed this awkward teenager into a young woman of astonishing wisdom.

Anne's spirit nets even the smallest butterfly of hope. Her capacity for love expands in captivity. In her silence she learns how to speak. A child's jottings become the description of a journey to be made by thousands of holocaust victims. Anne is able to turn deserts of despair into wellsprings of hope by her willingness to walk in the truth of who she is.

Women like Anne Frank prove that not even the cruelest suffering can daunt the power of a hopeful spirit. She would have found a soul-friend in another young woman, who, like herself, kept a diary and died in Auschwitz. Etty Hillesum writes of her experiences with a poignancy and accuracy few can match. In *An Interrupted Life*, her journal, and in her collected letters, we meet a lover of life, a scholar of refined sensitivity, a woman led by grace from doubt to belief. Etty tells of her choice to stay with her people rather than escape to freedom. Her candid, courageous spirit makes any other decision cowardly. Besieged Holland was and would remain her only home. Here, amidst the turbulence of Nazi tyranny, Etty finds that the only sane response to bleak despair is bright hope in the beauty of the human spirit. No amount of persecution can prevent its triumph. There are times, Etty says, when she lies awake at night on her bunk, feeling like a small pebble crushed by waves of human misery. Yet despite her tears she is able to rejoice in the extraordinary awareness that God is everywhere. The divine presence is like a flame that eternally catches fire, her faith like an underground spring that never ceases to flow. In one of her *Letters from Westerbork*, written on August 18, 1943, a few months before her death on November 30, Etty shares this graced insight with her friend Tide:

> This afternoon I was resting on my bunk and suddenly I just had to write these few words in my diary, and I now send them to you: "You have made me so rich, oh God, please let me share out your beauty with open hands. My life has become an uninterrupted dialogue with you, oh God, one great dialogue. Sometimes when I stand in some corner of the camp, my feet planted on your earth, my eyes raised toward your heaven, tears sometimes run down my face, tears of deep emotion and gratitude. At night, too, when I lie in my bed and rest in you, oh God, tears of gratitude run down my face, and that is my prayer. I have been terribly tired for

several days, but that too will pass. Things come and go in a deeper rhythm, and people must be taught to listen; it is the most important thing we have to learn in this life. I am not challenging you, oh God, my life is one great dialogue with you. I may never become the great artist I would really like to be, but I am already secure in You, God. Sometimes I try my hand at turning out small profundities and uncertain short stories, but I always end up with just one single word: God. And that says everything and there is no need for anything more. And all my creative powers are translated into inner dialogues with you. The beat of my heart has grown deeper, more active, and yet more peaceful, and it is as if I were all the time storing up inner riches."

In this private sharing Etty taps into the essence of what is good and holy in womanspirit. She lives in circles of communion inhabited by sisters in the spirit like Julian of Norwich, Teresa of Avila, and Thérèse of Lisieux. If we did not know her to be the author of the previous testimony of faith, hope, and love, we could easily imagine it to be theirs.

Julian's visions of redemptive suffering draw her into the epi-center of Christ's ignominious death and glorious resurrection. She refuses to flinch in the face of pain or to doubt the efficacy of God's gracious plan for her life. Comparable to Etty's uninterrupted dialogue with the holy is Julian's "showing" of a hazel nut:

He showed me a little thing, the size of a hazel nut, in the palm of my hand, and it was as round as a ball. I looked at it with my mind's eye and I thought, "What can this be?" And the answer came, "It is all that is made." I marvelled that it could last, for I thought it might have crumbled to nothing, it was so small. And the answer came into my mind, "It lasts and ever shall because God loves it." And all things have being through the love of God. In this little thing I saw three truths, the first is that God made it. The second is that God loves it. The third is that God looks after it. What is he indeed that is maker and lover and keeper? I cannot find words to tell. For until I am one with him I can never have true rest nor peace. I can never know it until I am held so close to him that there is nothing in between.

Julian's insights into the mystery of divine care shed light on a "vision of sorts" I once had. I was in my mid-twenties when this formative event took place. Life had come to one more crossroads in a series of appraisal moments. It was a confusing time for many. People my age were both dodging the draft and volunteering for service in Vietnam. Drugs were available on any street corner. Free sex was lauded as a welcome relief from stale morality. Talk of disease or danger was blithely dismissed as "old-fashioned." Here I was worrying about a commitment to teaching in the field of spiritual formation when the world was in chaos. Were my concerns real or imaginary? I had more questions than answers. Should I stay single or think about getting married? Would family life fit in with full-time ministry? Why was my faith so weak? Where would I be if I refused to open my heart and say yes always?

The sheer weight of what God might be asking of me was overwhelming. My focus was still far too narrow to grasp the personal message of scripture or to appreciate the wisdom of spiritual writers like Julian of Norwich. I remember for a split second matching the speed of my thoughts to the speed of my car. I caught myself just in time as I came over the crest of a hill and saw a delivery truck looming ahead of me at a slow pace. I slammed on the brakes, veered to the side of the road, and sat there stunned at my stupidity. I felt mad at myself, mad at the world, and, most of all, mad at God.

Suddenly, and for no apparent reason, it was as if these negative emotions were swept up in a whirlwind of positive energy. The surrounding hills almost went into a spin. I was lifted up like a pile of leaves caught in a spurt of fast-flowing air. The fallen leaves of my life seemed to be formed by grace into a new pattern. Sensations of movement and light engulfed me. For a split second, the blue of the sky was as intense as the bright orange of the sun. As when a car creeps to the top of a roller-coaster and careens over the edge, so I could not stop the rush of newfound trust I received. It was as if God had delivered me from doubt. I felt myself swimming in a sea of peace that calmed my futile concerns. I knew that none of this was of my doing. I was like a twig on the tide. What were my troubles compared to the vast treasury of God's tenacious love? What need was there for me to feel angry or anxious? Julian was the channel through whom I heard the words that described the mountaintop to which I had been led, albeit for a brief duration:

See, I am God. See I am in all things. See, I do all things. See, I never take my hands off my work, nor ever shall, through eternity. See, I lead all things to the end I have prepared for them. I do this by the same wisdom and love and power through which I made them. How can anything be done that is not well done?

The effects of this religious experience reverberate to this day in my mind and heart. Years have gone by since that near miss on the side of the road. What I learned then of God as maker, keeper, and lover sustains me still. Julian's confirming vision has since become my own: "All shall be well, and all shall be well, and all manner of thing shall be well." This prophecy is true. Another woman of wisdom, Teresa of Avila, showed me why trust in God's unfailing friendship is the surest wellspring of hope in a wounded world.

At a time when her shallow honor took precedence over her desire to follow God's invitation, Teresa claims to have seen hell itself in a horrifying vision of what life without divine friendship would be like. Hell was a place of agony, devoid of hope. Faced with the fundamental option to choose life or death, Teresa decided to allow grace to grind her precious honor to dust. She chose to let the Holy Spirit reshape her human spirit in the crucible of humility. Little proof would be forthcoming that she was living a life pleasing to God. How could she or anyone believe she was an instrument directed by the hand of a mighty composer? Was this tireless traveller, this poor sleeper, this whimsical writer really a future doctor of the church? All she did was initiate a reform few in authority took seriously. Covered with mud, suffering from severe migraines, suspect by the Inquisition, deterred from her mission by inexperienced spiritual guides, she is said to have challenged God, saying, "If this is the way you treat your friends, it's no wonder you have so few."

This haughty Spaniard had to find out the hard way that when everything looks bleak, humanly speaking, God is usually hardest at work. Such are the times grace chooses to draw willing spirits from winter to spring, from valleys of despair to vistas of hope. How could anyone seeing an ugly caterpillar believe it would turn into a beautiful butterfly? Or that a grain of sand invading an oyster's shell would become a shining pearl? Or that a spinning worm could produce fine silk? Yet Teresa witnessed such miracles of renewal in her own life.

Struggling to listen to God at the expense of her willfulness meant that she had to lay down her life in service of others. Losing her false, controlling self for the sake of finding her real self in Christ was torture for Teresa. Everything God wanted her to do turned out to be contrary to her own and others' expectations. For a while vanity blinded her to God's way of leading one across the moat of self-sacrifice to the castle of selfless love. Grace prompted her to move from refusal to surrender by means of prayer, conversations with holy people, sacred reading, and, in due time, solid spiritual direction. Only toward the end of her life did she come to see that "if one proceeds with detachment for God alone, there is no reason to fear that the effort will turn out bad; for [God] has the power to accomplish all."

As Teresa's prayer life undergoes a transformation from mediocrity to intimacy, she writes in Chapter 8 of the *Book of Her Life* about the tension between the two roads that diverge in her interiority — God awaiting her total abandonment to the mystery and the world beckoning her to rely on herself. For the longest time she could not grasp how to overcome this draining division in her inner life:

> for neither did I enjoy God nor did I find happiness in the world. When I was experiencing the enjoyments of the world, I felt sorrow when I recalled what I owed to God. When I was with God, my attachments to the world disturbed me. This is a war so troublesome that I don't know how I was able to suffer it even a month, much less for so many years.

She confesses with utter candor that for more than eighteen of the twenty-eight years since she had begun to pray in earnest, she suffered this split between friendship with God and flirtation with the ways of the world. Were these facets of her experience unalterably inimical to one another or was some reconciliation possible?

Teresa learns bit by bit that any attempt to separate God and the world will only result in a dualism contrary to the message of Christ and destructive of her mission. The enemy is not the world but an idolizing attachment forgetful of the truth, in her own words, that "God alone suffices." If all of life is a gift, an epiphany of God, then every manifestation of creation, human and cosmic, is a pointer beyond itself to the mystery of the "More Than." What appears at first glance to be a conflict is really a call to unity. As Teresa tells it in her *Spiritual Testimonies:*

> I was reflecting upon how arduous a life this is that deprives us of being always in that wonderful company [of God], and I said to myself, "Lord, give me some means by which I can put up with this life." He replied: "Think, daughter, of how after it is finished you will not be able to serve me in ways you can now. Eat for me and sleep for me, and let everything you do be for me, as though you no longer lived but I.... "

To mirror God's presence in our waking and resting, to be wholly with Christ in the world without being of the world, is not a distant possibility but the sole purpose of our existence. The earth and all that is in it is not an entity isolated from the eternal. It is the place where providence plays. It is our field of dreams and our chariot of fire.

One living flame was Thérèse of Lisieux. Her strength is mightier than her nickname, "The Little Flower," suggests. Shortly before her death in 1897, she had a remarkable vision. Dying of consumption, breathless with pain, Thérèse saw that she would soon take her seat at the celestial banquet. God would slake her thirst not with spoonfuls of milk but with the waters of eternal life. The more her disease drained her physical stamina, the stronger she grew in spirit. Her letters and last conversations reveal a desire to continue to work for the church and for the salvation of souls, if not on earth then in heaven. On July 14, 1897, she wrote to her confidante, Père Roulland:

> If I am leaving the battlefield this early, it is with no selfish desire to rest; the idea of eternal beatitude scarcely stirs a vibration in my heart; suffering has long been my heaven here below, and actually I find it hard to conceive how I shall get acclimatized in a Country where joy reigns with no tincture of sadness.... What attracts me to the Homeland of Heaven is the call of Jesus, the hope that I may at last love Him as I have so longed to love Him, and the thought that I shall bring a multitude of souls to love Him, who will bless Him for all eternity.

The strength of character and conviction shown by Thérèse throughout her final agony is a tribute to womanspirit. Rather than expecting her sisters to coddle her, she did all she could to encourage them to persevere in hope, to be of good cheer when death stopped at their door. With whatever energy she could muster, she chose to console them rather than wasting time feeling sorry for herself. In a moment of anguish on August 3, 1897, she asks for a scrap of paper on which she writes to her Sister Geneviève:

> O my God, how kind you are to the little victim of your merciful love. Now even when you add bodily suffering to my soul's anguish, I cannot say, "The sorrows of death surrounded me"; but I cry out in my gratitude "I have gone down into the valley of the shadow of death, yet will I fear no evil, for you, Lord, are with me!"

Moving ahead in time, I saw something of this spirit, this ability to transcend fear and the specter of hopelessness, in the faces of the women of Guadalupe. As I approached the shrine in Mexico City, I sensed the presence of the Spirit in these poor Indian peasants, to one of whom Mary had appeared. In rough clothing, down on their knees, they crossed the stony plaza carrying bouquets of roses to the Virgin. Their faith put to shame my petty claims to be spiritually mature. Admiration and gratitude of the same kind overtook me in East Africa. With infants on their backs and toddlers tugging at their skirts, the women of the villages walked for miles to worship with the men in makeshift churches. They sang in perfect harmony like choirs of angels. So radiant were their faces, so full of peace and joy, that for a moment I lost sight of their poverty and saw only the spiritual wealth that was theirs. Compared to them, I thought, what do we who come to minister have to bring but empty hands?

Anna, a Chinese woman, who used to be in charge of the cleaning crew on our floor of the college, had a face full of character, too, and the kindest smile. She never complains, I often thought. She accepts as her special duty to cheer up the faculty when we grimace cheerlessly. Marie, a woman in my parish, is another haven of hope. Rather than leaving her crippled daughter in a home under nurse's care, she treats her like any other child. Though she cannot move without a wheelchair, she takes her on trips to far away places like Alaska and Hawaii.

Women like these are a healing presence in an injured world. I need their witness to remain faithful to my own commitments. Once, walking along the Santa Barbara shore, I felt a wave of aloneness wash over me. I sensed sharply the sting of solitude. In the midst of musing about life's meaning, I stooped down and picked up what appeared to be a large stone. In reality it was a clump of small shells welded together by years of battering in the sea. Hundreds of small fragments like slivers of paper cut from life's harsh and happy seasons had been reshaped by nature and grace into a new whole. I went to the water's edge, washed off the excess grit, bounced the lump firmly a few times from hand to hand, and said to myself, "This could be my hazel nut." I mused, as Julian might, that life is not a haphazard collection of hapless bits. It is like this stone, made and kept and looked after by God. The clump rests now on my bookshelf. In my mind's eye it is an epiphany of the mystery, a sign of solidity signifying the hope of healing each time the whole of me has to endure yet another shattering.

It would be easy to slide down the slope of temptation, to begin to believe that life is a useless suffering. There are days when I, like you, feel abandoned by the mystery, as if the rock of my life were flung uncaringly into an indifferent universe. That is when I need to hold this ancient lump in the palm of my hand or raise it to my ear and listen, if only imaginatively, to the rush and roar of the sea. The result is awesome. This silent scrap becomes a messenger of the beyond. It reminds me, without my having to know why, that I must abandon myself to the mystery. As these small shells and sand grains surrendered to the vastness of the sea, only to be reshaped into an artwork in stone, so must I relinquish control over my destiny and trust the Master Sculptor to remake me into a new creation.

Once my two nephews, the older boy aged seven and the younger five at the time, knocked on Mother's door for a visit. There are two traits that characterize an Italian grandmother: love and food. It was her custom to lavish both on the boys. She gave them a bundle of hugs and kisses while they could smell chocolate chip cookies baking in the oven. Suddenly the older boy held up both hands and announced in determined tones, as if his dignity were at stake, "Grandmother, can't you see that I'm too old for this kind of mush." Then, pointing to his brother, he concluded,

"Give the hugs to him; he's only five and he needs them." Mother complied with this command, welcoming the younger boy with love pats and endearing words. Once more the action was put on hold as the older boy explained in no uncertain tones: "You realize, Grandmother, that this hugging arrangement has nothing to do with chocolate!"

The longing for "chocolate" is probably the last thing to die in us. We need a little consolation to get through our fear of loneliness. External bravado cannot cure a broken heart. We may pretend we can survive without a hug or two, but we only fool ourselves. A friend of mine says we need at least three serious hugs a day to survive — one each around breakfast, lunch, and dinner — to say nothing of several cookies of consolation from the jar in God's heavenly pantry!

Hope is a disposition that makes life worthwhile, even when no miracles happen. Hopeful hearts refuse to resign themselves to a predetermined fate. We must maintain a passion for the impossible like Maxie does. While working as a Peace Corps volunteer in Brazil, she contracted a rare and debilitating tropical disease. Despite occasional loss of muscle and speech control, she continues to study for her Ph.D. in psychology. She is a living example of the old saying: "When the going gets tough, the tough get going." Her hope for the future does not depend on horoscopic predictions but in doing the best she can hour by hour, day by day, to be faithful to God's plan for her life. She does not hope in the possible, which is under human control, but in the impossible, which is under the canopy of divine providence.

There are days in everyone's life when it feels as if the race is over before the runners leave the starting line. Hope can be as fragile as a thread. We need to be on the alert for signs that a shift is occurring. A day will come when God shatters the silence and addresses to our hearts a word of hope. A pebble of insight rolls onto the shore. Dawn breaks after a midnight that never seems to end. Light appears just as we despair of the darkness ever passing. That of which I speak is not evident in a world impatient for instant solutions. It is not a possession we can trade like a stock market commodity.

Hope is not a product of human power. It frequently hides its face behind the mask of failure or poverty. It crops up unexpectedly when dreams collapse. Hope is apt to appear over the next horizon when our best laid plans fall apart like burnt embers. Hope hangs on like a long lost relative who refuses to leave a week after the family reunion is over. It is like a dry creek that fills up during a sudden downpour. After her husband was killed in a plane crash, Betty refused to see anyone. Her grief was too overwhelming. For months she put off accepting any invitation, sought no counseling, went through the motions of her work but without heart. The day she finally gave her dead husband's shirts to Good Will was the day I knew her hope in life had been restored.

When we hope against hope, when we refuse to let daily routines become unbearable burdens, when we accept life's limits as God's special gifts, we experience what it feels like to be free. We become like lighthouses sending signals to storm-tossed ships. Ports of call are always within reach if we keep scanning the horizon. Hope convinces us that a safe harbor is nearby. It does not rest on the loose sand of human whims but on the firm foundation of God's solicitude, which no storm, however fierce, can sweep away.

The roots of our hope sink into the rich soil of appreciative abandonment to the ultimately benevolent way in which the Holy Spirit guides our life. Hope is our answer as Christians to the seeming silence of God. It is an act of supreme confidence, in the face of sin and depression, in the saving power of Jesus Christ. We believe that our help is in the name of the Lord, who has made heaven and earth.

Hope counteracts the narcissistic expectation that life will succumb to "Control Center Me." It sidetracks our disrespectful, prideful attempts to master the mystery. It focuses not on human willfulness but on the wisdom of God. It refuses to take refuge in scornful pessimism but points instead to the evidence of salvation history. Hope checks our urgency to rewrite God's script. It encourages us to trust in a reality that infinitely transcends our narrow vision.

In the down hours, when I come to the end of my "hope-rope," I accept the necessity of reaching out for help. I call a friend, reserve a table at a restaurant that lifts my spirits, leave my desk and go for a long walk. I force my frowning face to break into smiles at the slightest excuse. I fake laughter until tears of mirth become real. I remember the words of Gregory of Nyssa: "Hope always draws the soul from the beauty which is seen to what is beyond, always kindles the desire for the hidden through what is constantly perceived."

Hope reminds me that there is power in powerlessness, energy in patient endurance, joy underneath mantles of pain. I think of hope not as a disposition peculiar to believing Christians but as a duty in the present age. All around us we see signs of the lingering disease of sexual and racial discrimination. We witness, often in our own family, the raw wounds of marital infidelity or aborted love affairs. The senseless waste of drug and alcohol abuse is statistically on the rise among women. The recurrent threat of war and nuclear devastation fills the media. Is it not clear that women, as life-givers and life-bearers, have a duty to rekindle hope in a dying hearth of hopelessness? I wish hope were a luxury for the spiritually elite, but it is increasingly a survival measure in the modern world.

Without hope of this heart-wrenching sort, we might only live what Henry David Thoreau named "lives of quiet desperation." Look at the faces of the people who rush through airports or file into rapid rise elevators as if they were operating on automatic pilot. Many already seem to be victims of a play of forces over which they have no control. They posture a fatalistic philosophy, convinced that their best efforts can change nothing, certainly not the destructive, oppressive weights that trap women and men in vice-like grips of submission and domination.

Hope empowers us, as no other disposition of the heart can, to change death to life, sorrow to joy, desperation to delight. Hope points us toward an opportunity for transformation when nothing but obstacles seem to block our way. What is hope if not the assurance that the soup tastes good despite the hair on our spoon, that the marble is lovelier because of the flaws in it?

Once, shortly after she had lectured to her nuns on the necessity of penance and detachment for the sake of purity of heart, Teresa of Avila heard a knock on the convent's kitchen door. A hunter wanted to present the sisters with a lovely brace of partridge for their supper. The dilemma was apparent. Despite the rules of fasting the nuns followed, they could not stop their mouths from watering at the thought of tasting these succulent little birds. With her usual aplomb, Teresa solved the problem. This master of mortification is reported to have said: "My dears, my dears, will you never learn! In the house of our gracious God, in this humble abode where the divine name is holy, the answer is obvious: 'Penance is penance, and partridge is partridge, so by all means, let's enjoy a good meal.' " For a woman whose high mystical graces did not quell her longing to savor a little sardine, it should come as no surprise that hers, as the poet Alexander Pope said, is a human breast in which "hope springs eternal." Teresa combined the certitude of confidence in God alone with the effectiveness of down-to-earth works of mercy and charity. She is a model of openness to the mystery of formation revealing itself in the arena of daily reality.

We have nothing to lose and everything to gain by emulating Teresa's conviction that waiting in patience attains to all things. The more ours becomes a story of hope, the better our chances become to change the course of history. What women want in the way of world renewal is not cosmetic change but transformation in depth. The energy we need to effect personal and societal restructuring has to emerge from the ground of undying faith and hope — the kind of hope that enabled the early Christian community to flourish despite persecution and no initial evidence of anything but defeat.

We must remain women of the world, rational and active, responsible for good works and coherent strategies, women whose plans for the future are constructive and whose predictions are positive. But, as women of faith, we must also be like what Evelyn Underhill calls amphibious creatures living with one foot in time and the other in eternity. Our hearts must be attuned, as finely as violin strings, to the foolishness of the cross, lest we become so activistic and efficient that we forget to acknowledge our dependence on God.

We cannot build our future without remembering our past. This means that we have to take into account women's contributions to the course of history while tracing the causes of cruelty that would kill the spirit. What is required by the rule of hope is that we do the best we can to bring to fruition the present hour of social and spiritual awakening. Women's concerns for church and society have led us individually and collectively to the edge of a new era of equality and respect for each person's dignity and gifts. Our hope for a better tomorrow depends on what enspirited women do today. We trust that what we have started in this time of transition will set the tone for the next two thousand years of womanly and manly Christian witness.

Happy, indeed, is she to whom it is given
to share this sacred banquet,
to cling with all her heart to [Jesus]
whose beauty all the heavenly hosts admire
unceasingly,
whose love inflames our love,
whose contemplation is our refreshment,
whose gentleness fills us to overflowing,
whose remembrance brings a gentle light,
whose fragrance will revive the dead,
whose glorious vision will be the happiness
of all the citizens of the heavenly Jerusalem.
— *Clare of Assisi*

11

Carriers of the
Christian Faith Tradition

*B*EING CATHOLIC, as I know from my own and others' experience, is not a casual matter. Whether we stay in the church as routine Mass-goers, leave in protest only to return the wiser, or say good-bye forever, this faith and formation tradition impacts so strongly on our psyche and spirit that there is no escaping its influence.

"Once a Catholic, always a Catholic." I used to think that phrase was exaggerated until I began talking to women and hearing their testimonials. One can be in the church and secretly hate it or outside the church and secretly love it, but one cannot be indifferent to it. We may despise institutional hypocrisy while feeling empathy for the church's earthly brokenness, but we can never totally escape our ecclesial roots. The thumbprint of tradition presses too deeply. For better or worse the church is in our individual and collective consciousness.

For years, when I taught full-time at Duquesne University, whose campus is adjacent to downtown Pittsburgh, I would stop in the morning at one of the old churches near Point State Park for Mass or to say a prayer before the Blessed Sacrament. Religious anthropologists like Mircea Eliade describe the threshold experience of passing from secular to sacred space. I sensed that passage when I stepped from a busy intersection into the dim blue light of the sanctuary, smelled the peculiarly Catholic odor of melting wax and incense, saw the lifesize statues of saints like the "Little Flower," and watched the faces of the people who came to daily services. The routine was as comforting and restorative as the rituals themselves. This year-by-year unfolding of the liturgical calendar was as sure as the seasons. It sustained me through many difficult moments. I liked dropping a few coins in the metal container, hearing the click of copper against brass, and lighting a candle. I remembered what the sisters taught me in grade school: that the whiff of smoke would carry my prayer to the heavens long after I left the church. What a comforting thought it was to believe that a vaporous element like candle smoke could continue praying for me when I was lost in functional space, separated from eternity by clock time.

In the early morning, under the scarf of an old lady, I would catch an imaginary glimpse of my own grandmother. I would see in the gnarled fingers of this archetypal candle lighter thousands of women like her who chose to set wicks aflame in faith rather than to curse the darkness. I would wait for the clink of her coin and wonder to which of the many unlit tapers she would touch the flame. All of them looked the same to me, but not to her. She always chose the third candle from the top directly in front of the crucifix. She seemed visibly upset when it happened already to be lit. Would its smoke ascend more swiftly than that of another? Once the flame sputtered upward, she would kneel, knees cracking, and pray perhaps a decade of the rosary. Once when I was rushing and had only a minute, I wondered: "What will it be like when all I have left is the energy to light one candle?" Would such an act be merely a surface gesture or would it be for another's eye evidence of true faith?

I had been away from town for almost the entire summer. When I returned in September to school, I resumed the routine of stopping by the old church to pray and, as was by now my custom, to light a few candles. The minute I crossed the threshold I knew something was amiss. While the smell of incense still clung to the walls, the waxy scent was faint to nonexistent. Then I saw in a disbelieving flash why this was so. The candles had all but disappeared in a wash of electronic efficiency. Someone had replaced them with push-button electric lights that would burn for a pre-designated moment and then, on their own accord, unaffected by wind or cold, human breath or the flutter of passing bodies, switch off.

This concession to fire safety or ease in cleaning or cost-effectiveness or whatever reason might have been given by whatever parish committee cut into my heart. I felt as if the outside world of steel and granite had invaded this sacred space like a cloud of industrial smoke chokes off pure air. How could they do such a thing? Was no one aware of the power of symbol? Could a tiny bulb send up smoke on clouds of angels' wings? Could an electric charge carry my prayers to the ears of God as well as a whiff of smoke?

What happened might have been to any other beholder an insignificant event, but for me it had wider implications. I already feared the paucity of symbols in our "plastic" world and the effect of such erosion on people's faith. I wanted the church to respond to the signs of the times, especially where women's issues were concerned, but without losing its symbolic capacity to address the heart. I wanted to preserve the feeling, borne by sacred symbols, of the church's being a home where world-weary pilgrims could rest and relish a moment of peace.

I realize that what had occurred was in my mind a violation of a space that had become a special spiritual oasis. Someone had moved in and remodeled my "home" without consulting me about the new plans, and I felt betrayed. It was not only the disappearance of candles that evoked my silent protest; it was the whole mentality of functional efficiency eroding transcendent possibility that frightened me. Stripping away this symbol was tantamount to destroying something treasured solely for reasons of the heart. It was like burning a person's love letters without asking because they cluttered up the bureau drawer.

I got over the initial impact of what was for me a violent alteration of sacred space. I even continued stopping by the church on a morning or evening, but I never "pushed on a light." I noticed also that the old woman did not press the third button below the center of the shiny new crucifix, never to be blackened by beeswax. Life stays the same. Life inexorably changes. What lasts? What remains essential in woman's understanding of the church? Here is one answer:

Over the years of attending the liturgy, seeing the example of priests and religious, being supported in my faith by family and other relationships, doing my reading, I have developed some understanding of what it can mean to allow Jesus to be the center of my doing, thinking and being. Being a Catholic is not easy. At times I feel frustrated, confused, and discouraged, but I also receive real blessings from God, from the Mass and the sacraments. Without my church I would not be the person I am, nor would I trust in the Lord and look forward to becoming a citizen of heaven.

Women and men of faith believe there is a direct link between life in the present and our hope of things to come. For me, the candle was a symbol of earth, of things made that are precious but ever passing. Life itself is consumed like wax in fire, transformed by nature from what is solid to what goes up in smoke. This is the way of the world — nothing is lasting, all is passing, moving, changing. Faith teaches that this "between time" has a profound purpose — to prepare us for what is to come, our citizenship in heaven.

These may sound like words from a catechism of old, their ring may be too otherworldly, but they capture what Rosemary Haughton calls the "catholic thing." This longing for the More Than, this sense that a restless heart only rests in God, this looking forward to a time when all shall be well and every tear shall be wiped away (Rev. 21:4) portends the banquet table prepared for us from the beginning. Our "catholic thing" tells us that this promise shall come to pass, provided Jesus is the center of our life. He is the rock to which we cling in storms that rage. He is the saving One whose healing power binds what is broken and puts balm on every wound.

•

I am in Munich in one of those cavernous German cathedrals that, like so many Catholic architectural masterpieces, have become almost museums. Groups of tourists form traffic patterns that weave meticulously from the entrance of the church to the altar. Hums of appreciation rise and fall as the guide conveys yet another fact of history. I watch this interplay for a while, resisting the attraction to tag along. Instead I seek a quiet place. I need a moment of peace, a healing glance at the heavenly citizenry.

The day before I had been in Dachau for the first and what may be the last time, so shaken was I by the stark horror of a concentration camp. Even the presence of a Carmelite monastery on the grounds of this hell of hate did not cushion the shock of standing where so many had perished, inch by inch of their dignity stripped away like paint on old furniture ready to be thrown into the fire. These victims of man's inhumanity to man were treated like herds of cattle, not people created in God's image. No one respected these innocent victims as future citizens of heaven. They lived the cross as much as Jesus did, whether they knew he was with them in Dachau or not. There was no way to endure such a scene except in faith — a faith as naked as the women and men who were sent into the gas chambers ostensibly to take a shower.

As I walked over the gravel damp with morning dew, moving in silence through the barracks where human beings had been racked like slabs of meat, I shook with disbelief. Was Sartre right after all? Were we only wolves who preyed upon the weak? Was there no meaning to life beyond the grave? Then the smoke was violent, not gentle. It emanated from burning bodies. It rose reluctantly to the heavens from the chimneys of ovens symbolizing the result of absolute power that corrupts absolutely.

What weeping must have wet these stones, though waterfalls of tears could not quench the fires of such hate. Where was God amidst this devastation? Had the light ceased to shine? Or could it glow in the darkness and the darkness grasp it not?

The hum of the tour groups faded into the background as they went down into the church's crypt. I found a quiet corner to pray before the altar of the Blessed Virgin. I saw a serene statue with sad eyes darkened by the smoke of candles burning beneath it. Spontaneously I dropped in a coin, lit a taper, and watched the wisp wind upward. I imagined it mingling with the air over Dachau that wafted the death by burning of holocaust victims heavenward. Mary's inner directed eyes gave me hope. She saw what I could only imagine. Had not her own son, too, died in Dachau? Does he not die again everywhere in the world where humans are victims of their own kind? And does he not rise in them like incense burning?

Before the statue, watching my candle catch fire with a brighter flame, I knew I had to make yet another leap of faith. I had to abandon myself to the mystery of God's sustaining, ultimately benevolent love, to forgive what I had seen while vowing in my own small way to prevent such an atrocity from ever happening again. I wanted what I was feeling before this altar in Munich to flow into the world outside the church's door, for I, too, share a woman's belief

> ... that the embrace of the Catholic church includes all people, indeed, all of creation. For me the Incarnation of Jesus Christ is God's way of embracing all of humanity inclusively. The way I see it, human beings participate in or are conscious of participating in the community of God in different ways and in differing degrees, but God's universal — or catholic — love embraces all.

The image of an embrace is a frequent metaphor women use to describe the church. It was as if Julian of Norwich saw God's hands literally holding the earth as one might grip a hazel nut about to fall and break in two. How much more comforting it is to think of the church as a nurturing mother rather than a stern taskmaster. The same woman continues:

> To me the institution we call "church" is only one dimension, one expression of the Catholic community in its universal totality. Participation in the institutional church does influence my life. It is the way in which I am reminded day by day of the primacy of my relationship with God ... of my essential connection to God. It is a reminder to live that relationship lovingly; it makes God real for me.

I am in another church ... this time in downtown Manhattan. It is a mission chapel in the middle of the world's biggest, most competitive marketplace. It smells of incense and candlewax. One or the other religious order priest hears confessions for twelve hours of the twenty-four. When I arrive around three in the afternoon several people are already in line. I almost forget to examine my own conscience as I become absorbed in the faces and figures seeking reconciliation with God, needing through word and blessing to reconnect with others.

Consciousness of my own sins and the wideness of God's mercy enables me to feel sympathy for the executive who brings his briefcase with him into the box. Perhaps it needs to be blessed as much as he does. I behold the stirring of sorrow for sin in the heavily made up matron whose lips never stop moving. Is there no one else with whom she can converse but herself and God? I wonder what is wrong with the street kid dressed in jeans spare at the knees, wringing his hands and looking worried. All wait for the priest to listen and allay their fears.

In this mission church I have found the "salt of the earth" of Catholic life. Meditating upon the faces of the people standing in line, soon to receive communion, I feel tears welling up in my eyes. I see the church at this moment as a mother who welcomes strangers, relieves their loneliness, and makes them feel part of the family. I understand as the lines progress past my pew that everyone, from the corporate officer to the street urchin, is in God's eyes a distinctively human, uniquely spiritual being created in the divine image and form with inner beauty and dignity. Each is worthy to be numbered among the people of God. Each deserves the titles: royal, priestly, prophetic. This is the church without walls, the church unlimited by sociological statistics. This is the eucharist of everydayness, the place of grace where God in Christ welcomes to the same banquet table without discrimination the designer-clad career woman and the lady dressed in rags, the mother hushing children and the grandmother kneeling alone.

I pretend there is a fleck of dust in my eye to hide my emotion. The woman next to me digs a wrinkled Kleenex out of her purse and says, "Don't worry, honey, it's clean." I try to stop the tears, but it's not easy. This entire motley crew of Christians is my people. It is as if we are on a ship in danger of sinking, though none of us want to abandon her for a variety of reasons. In the words of a director of religious education:

> The church gives me a framework by which to relate to the world. It provides guidance, a way of interpretation, a challenge, a balance. It calls me to be universal in my love. As a woman religious, I am aware of representing the church by the habit I wear. Ministering here in the South, for instance, I sense daily the need to be ecumenical. When I am in a Jewish community, I try to be conscious of my *Judeo* roots as well. My awareness is related to *where* I am and who I am *with* rather than to any rigid clinging to my catholicity as such.

This commitment to revere all people in Christ's name creates a climate of sensitivity for the world and its inhabitants. Women fight to preserve our ecology. On Earth Day 1990, a woman in Nairobi organized an action to keep the central park there an oasis of natural beauty rather than converting it into an industrial complex. Whole groups of women and men joined the action to have tuna harvested without trapping and killing dolphins in the same nets. The effort to care for the ecology of this planet, this thrust toward global oneness, makes religious prejudice and the wars it promotes increasingly scandalous. Christ's blessing on the peacemakers, his calling us children of God, arouses a longing in women to lead the way to a new era of interconnectedness, to a being *with* nature, *with* other women and men in mutuality and partnership. This desire undercuts differences that divide us from one another and from the cosmos. It arouses in every reflective person a transcendent longing for union and communion, bonding and belonging, conserving and protecting.

•

What the young catechist did not know, what no one in the orientation sessions could cover in detail, were the customs of the people, the harshness of their life in these remote Mexican mountain villages. Being missioned here had taught her in short order that faith was alive among the poor, that they would teach her more than she could tell them. The air in the hills was pure, the food simple and nourishing. She had begun to thrive on beans and rice, spring water and an occasional mug of beer. Mass every Sunday in this region would have been an unheard-of luxury. When the people knew a priest was coming to celebrate the sacred mysteries, they would travel long distances by foot and on donkeys to be there. It was as if they were pilgrims on their way to Canterbury for a grand festival.

The atmosphere in the village of choice would be charged with excitement. The children would run around like chickens, their voices rising like gusts of wind. The women would make cornmeal cakes. The men would come in early from the fields, wash and put on fresh clothes to make the journey. If their village was designated as the site of the eucharistic celebration, they would set up the altar on a knoll outside the town. Hundreds of peasants might be there, many of whom had had no opportunity to receive communion for weeks. The catechist had an inkling of what would occur from volunteers who had served in these parts previously, but no one had prepared her for the ceremony of the bugs.

At first she thought the people were carrying jars of corn kernels until she detected the squirming movements. There were as many jars as there were peasants who transported them. They spread them row by row in front of and around the sides of the altar like candle pots without a wick. The jars were closed but that did not detract from the unusual spectacle. She sought an explanation. The village elder chuckled and asked her forgiveness for not explaining earlier.

"You see, Miss, the peasants know from experience that every seven years or so these bugs, who have also to eat, choose our corn as food. These are not good bugs. They do not have to eat of our livelihood. We are of the belief that if these bad bugs line up in the presence of the living God, if they are blessed by the Padre's hand, they will go somewhere else for their meal. How could bugs so blessed refuse to obey?"

The priest came and offered Mass in the open air under a bright blue sky. Earth blended with the heavens as bread and wine became the body and blood of Christ. Voices rose and fell in festive song. The Mass came alive for her in a wonderful way. She felt in her heart what faith in the face of human pain could mean. After communion, as if the priest knew instinctively what had to be done to respect the cosmic wonder of the people, he initiated the ceremony of the blessing of the bugs. He asked the creatures to be kind to the faithful and to find a remote place to feed, away from the crops the villagers were tending. He tried not to condemn the bugs as such. They did not know they were being so bad. He asked only that they respect this request of the living God.

By custom the people left the jars at the altar and went home singing. Later the village boys and girls disposed of them by placing the jars in nearby caves, sealed tight by many stones. The catechist observed in due time that the corn crop in the region was especially abundant that year. Was it because the bugs were buried or because they were blessed? What did it matter? Mother Nature had made peace with the people. The villagers had more stories to pass on to their children about the power of the Most High. "This is truly church," thought the catechist. "I would not trade this moment for a glamorous time in the greatest city on earth." Later she wrote to me:

> I am learning again, thanks to these people, that the Catholic church in many ways is like a parent. You are born into it and to them. They have been sent by God to nourish, protect,

guide, feed, and launch their children in life.... Why am I a Catholic? Why do I believe in this faith tradition? Why do both church and family hold authority over me? Both should and do have my love and respect. For my part... I must answer to Christ. I am responsible for my relationship with the Lord, with the earth, with everyone I meet.

In a slightly different vein, a priest friend said to me: "I am amazed that grown men, executives and lawyers, that grown women, medical doctors and technicians, still confess as if they were children. It is like listening to twelve-year-olds. People grow in every other way, but their relationship with God seems to stop in early adolescence."

The image of church as parent (Mother Church, Father Church), of us as children, has a gentle as well as a firm side. When I was a little girl and felt sick, I liked being served breakfast in bed. I needed mothering. We all do at times. Comparing the church to a "mother" suggests that she heals sinful hearts, lifts failing spirits, satisfies hunger, nurtures new life. Comparing the church to a "father" calls to mind one whose authority we are taught to obey, whose hand guides us firmly through the present and into the future, though not with overbearing power. Lest the analogy become overly dualistic, it is clear that both parents are at times forgiving and stern, providing answers and giving us room to take responsibility for our life. Autonomy is as necessary for growth as authority. Arguments that are adolescent need not replace fruitful dialogues between adults. When factions stop quarreling like children intent on having their own way, reforms can occur, foundations of faith can be retained, with no loss of respect on either side.

Like a wise parent, the church ought not to shun any of its children. Some have walked out of the house and slammed the door behind them, but this is not the way of the Spirit. As one woman said:

> I think of the Roman Catholic church as a melding of widely varying viewpoints and cultures brought together under one banner. The church continues to grow and thrive precisely to the extent of its willingness to accommodate a wide diversity of people and points of view while maintaining its sense of mission, its splendid vision.

The walls of churches may be made of cement, but they ought to be treated like rubber. Rubber stretches and bends. It expands to include many nations, races, and traditions under one roof. To another woman, "The church as 'catholic' means an all-embracing, understanding instrument of God's love for us."

> It does affect my life and the decisions I make. . . . Many times I have to defend a teaching with which I do not agree because that is how it is. This does not mean a law or custom feels good to everyone or that it is free of double standards.

•

> As a black woman and a religious, I sometimes believe that the church does not address me at all, as if I am in a void. Once, a long time ago, I left parish life and tried to affiliate with another denomination. . . . I thought I could feel at home there, but I really could not overcome my longing for the liturgy, for the tradition and history of Catholicism, its consistency and the universality of its teaching.

Her image of church, despite experiences of alienation, is still one of homecoming, but this is not always the case. As another woman observes:

> I had seven children in nine years while I was married to an alcoholic. The rigidity of the church's teaching on birth control and divorce was destructive to my life and the lives of my children. But the casualness of divorce today is at least as destructive. What is right? What is wrong? I do know that I must try to make every decision in the light of biblical teaching and the basic message of Christ to love and serve one another.

Faith prevails in the face of ambiguity. The death-to-life message of the scriptures offsets the temptation to despair when outmoded customs block creative approaches to change. To trim dead branches does not destroy a tree. What is rigid snaps off anyway. Trees less weighed down by dry wood flex in the wind. They are less likely to blow over because their roots go deep into the earth. So it is with the church.

Our tradition is anchored in the firm soil of gospel truth, watered by the underground spring of eucharistic grace. There could be no more solid foundation upon which to grow. Fears of entering into relationships of cooperation and mutual respect must be set aside as women and men pursue the common good in service of Christ's way. Exemplary is this woman's story of an adult conversion experience:

> At the time I was living in the southern part of the United States ... regularly attending Mass at a Catholic church and also attending Bible classes for single adults at a local Baptist congregation. Most of my friends were members of the latter, though many had been raised in other denominations. About three years after my conversion experience, I began to feel the fullness of what the church meant to me. I had been raised Catholic as had my father and his family. My mother was a convert, who treasured her new found spiritual home. I had attended Catholic schools for most of my life. To leave the church would in many ways be like leaving a mother. She was vital to my formation ethically, culturally, intellectually, and liturgically. I knew it would hurt my parents if I left. One of my brothers had done so already, and his decision was a source of family conflict from time to time. It was too difficult for me to think about this question, so I brought it to prayer. From within my heart the answer arose. As much as I loved and admired the fervor of my friends, the directive I received was unambiguous. "Stay where you are."

I remember talking to a sister friend of mine who told me that in the course of three years, four women from her novitiate class of seven had left the congregation. Each time one friend departed, she asked herself, "Why should I stay? What does my vocation mean?"

Each time I attend a liturgy where the priest mumbles the Mass or speeds through the prayers as if a traffic cop were chasing him, I too wonder why so many Catholics keep coming back to parishes where little or no formation occurs. What is it that holds us when it would be so tempting to leave?

> I understood when I heard the words, 'stay where you are' that Jesus was the most important person in my life. ... I also realized that I was to continue living out my faith, my spiritual life, within the context of this two thousand year tradition. I could not take what I had received for granted; neither could I deny the awareness of the Bible, the teaching and fellowship, I had received from the Baptist congregation. I had to shape

my life in dialogue with the church, but I had to be free to seek certain truths and experiences outside the church. . . . What remains most important to me — the great gift of Catholicism — is the sacramental life and, especially, the Eucharist. This is my way of worship, but like many women I suffer because my gifts are overlooked; my call to discipleship is diminished.

As I know from our correspondence, it is not this woman's style either to sit on the sidelines or to join a chorus of complainers. She continues to be a go-getter and is already known in her parish as a leader. She continues to study theology and spirituality, to facilitate prayer groups, to do vocational counseling, and to read scripture and the writings of the masters for personal and spiritual enrichment.

Without belligerence, holding firm to her beliefs, she bides her time, neither resisting the authority and direction of the church nor succumbing to bitterness because she experiences at times being a stranger in her own house. Though it is difficult in this age of individuation to find a community of believers, especially for lay persons, she tries to encourage new models of faithful living and seeks support where she can find it, mainly in small Christian groups. Her friendships, her ministry and sense of apostolic zeal, her discipleship and teaching are influenced as much by the church as by other professionals, both Christians and non-Christians.

Recently she wrote:

We live in tense times, but I try to remain thankful for all that God has done for me uniquely and for us as a community of believers. I appreciate myself as a woman, as a single Catholic professional, who believes in a life of prayer and a passion for service. In this I identify with other Christian women, Catholic or not. The decisions I make are rarely, if ever, in conflict with essential church teachings. Doctrine is seldom the problem. Certain practices I find more alienating than affirming. Once a group of seven of us, single women, myself included, wanted to buy tickets for a parish dance. We were refused admission because we would be attending as a group, not as couples, for none of us were dating. I heard later that some of the married women felt threatened by the presence of so many single women at the dance. I almost gave up at that point, wondering what life in an average parish held in store for me. Even though I knew that the pastor did not always know what to make of me, I stayed on, and for this grace I am grateful. At least we now have a good program in place to minister to singles. I consider this a sign of progress, don't you?

Rather than answering her question directly, and in fairness to the voices of women that have been heard throughout this book, I would like to propose in my next chapter an imaginative dialogue between womanspirit and the church from whence we may draw our own conclusions.

12 ❧

The church is in the world to save the world. It is a tool of God for that purpose; not a comfortable religious club established in fine historical premises.

— *Evelyn Underhill*

A Conversation between Womanspirit and the Church

WOMANSPIRIT: May I begin this dialogue by saying with appreciation and affection that you make my life difficult and you make it immensely worthwhile.

CHURCH: Shall we begin by tackling what is troublesome?

WOMANSPIRIT: This talk depends on our mutual willingness to take a realistic look at the way we live our faith and struggle daily with moral dilemmas. Ours must be a spirituality based not only on fixed rules and regulations but on the love, acceptance, and forgiveness exemplified by Christ.

CHURCH: That is our hope as well but, alas, we often fall short. Behind a humble façade hide hypocrisy and self-righteousness. Such is the human condition; yet we are called by Christ's example to love our neighbor as we love ourselves.

WOMANSPIRIT: Our faith tradition challenges us to greatness. It calls us to go beyond self-centered inclinations and attend to communal needs. The church is the channel through which the Spirit speaks. The Eucharist is the privileged place of our relation to God. Our catholicity is an essential component of who we are.

CHURCH: Being Catholic truly affects every facet of our life and all of our decisions, doesn't it?

WOMANSPIRIT: There is no way I can deny this truth. You are my home, my family, the community into which I was born and nurtured, the place of God where I have lived and will one day die. But like a family where no member is perfect, you, too, have your strengths and weaknesses.

CHURCH: Meaning?

WOMANSPIRIT: You are both loving and hurtful to your children, accepting and rejecting, encouraging and critical, gentle and harsh. At times your all-too-human side is more apparent to people than that which is divinely inspired.

CHURCH: Is the latter so difficult to see?

WOMANSPIRIT: The likeness to Christ is sometimes hard to behold.

CHURCH: Of what shortcomings would you speak?

WOMANSPIRIT: Naming specifics is not my purpose. I would only ask for profound self-examination and conversion of heart: Do you act in such a way as to embrace the whole family of God? Do you teach this truth by deed, not in word only?

CHURCH: You mean as Jesus did?

WOMANSPIRIT: He is the model we must follow. He was neglected and scorned, yet he never ceased to love and forgive, even his betrayers. He was God, yet he did not use his divinity to gain power over others but to reveal what it means to be a servant-leader. First he healed and forgave, then he said to sin no more.

CHURCH: How awesome was the depth of his love!

WOMANSPIRIT: He had a way of accepting persons as they were, not swiftly judging. He loved the sinner while hating the sin. People felt he knew them as they were with their special gifts. He befriended women and chose them as his disciples. He was interested in addressing deeper needs. He cared for souls, not money. He knew when and why people were hurting, and he did all that he could to give them hope.

CHURCH: What a challenge it is to bring the gospel to the whole world!

WOMANSPIRIT: When you address people's deepest needs with love, they will respond and become more of what God intended them to be. Hearts will be converted. Oppression will cease. Justice will be done. Women will weep less for their children. They will feel accepted, respected, loved, and called forth to use their gifts for the glory of God. With such an aura of care and concern surrounding us, there will be no reason for women or men to rebel. War will seem increasingly ridiculous, especially when it is waged in religion's name. Putting self first will make no sense. Resentment and rejection will give way to reconciliation and respect.

CHURCH: All will begin to unfold according to God's plan...

WOMANSPIRIT: Yes, as the Holy Trinity intended from the beginning. ... Sin obscures our vision as God's people, but Christ has saved us from such poor sight. You must help us to behold God with unveiled faces. Then we cannot help but submit freely and with joy to your age-old wisdom and authority.

CHURCH: Such openness is the ideal...

WOMANSPIRIT: In this light to shun any gift is to risk violating God's will, but women are patient. We are able to persist against great odds. We know what it means to enter into the long process of birth, to make and keep friendships that endure, to embrace spouses and children when they would otherwise feel abandoned. We know what it means with hands and hearts and voices to express compassion for our own and others' vulnerability.

CHURCH: Your care in Christ's name has carried us over the centuries. ...

WOMANSPIRIT: We are caregivers, instruments of God's love and healing in a broken world. There is too much to be done for us to turn back merely because we have been treated in demeaning ways or told to return with our requests another day.

CHURCH: You always come back...

WOMANSPIRIT: Because we belong to the one true fold, ... because we are in a time of transition to the next two thousand years of Christianity, ... because we must together pass gospel values on to the next generation. Women are tradition bearers, but we are not afraid to rock the boat.

CHURCH: But what if the ship begins to sink...

WOMANSPIRIT: We would be the first to bale. We may be pressing the boundaries of renewal, but we would never abandon ship. We wish clergy would be more understanding. We would like to be accepted on our own terms. Men must cease behaving as if we were threats. Such childish responses to reform are unnecessary among friends and co-workers. Jesus has freed us from succumbing to craven fears.

CHURCH: We must look to him always for guidance...

WOMANSPIRIT: And to Mary. With great courage, in response to God's call, she accepted to mother the savior of the world. Later he met another Mary, sister of his friend, Martha. Both women, one contemplative, the other more active, were loved by him, both became disciples, followers, in the deepest sense. He made still another Mary, the Magdalene, the announcer of his resurrection. And Mary of Bethany washed his feet. He accepted water from an outcast, a woman of Samaria, and saved another, condemned for adultery, from being stoned. A woman with a hemorrhage touched his garment's hem and received healing. Veronica wiped his bleeding face. And he told the women who wailed along death's route to weep not for him but for their children.

CHURCH: What do you conclude in the light of these events?

WOMANSPIRIT: It is not conclusions I would draw but a new vision. Mary bathes his feet with her tears and perfumes them with precious ointments while Judas, his betrayer, castigates this waste and hypocritically says the money paid for such extravagance could have been given to the poor. Veronica wipes his battered brow as he struggles toward Golgotha while all around him men jeer and one has to be coaxed to help him lift high the cross. And who but the women prepared his body for burial? The men had gone into hiding for fear they would be arrested.

CHURCH: The evidence of his making women partners in the mystery of redemption is convincing, to be sure.

WOMANSPIRIT: Mary is the new Eve. She is first among women. She is the strongest warrior of us all, yet she stays gentle as a dove. Capable of crushing the head of the serpent, she remains self-effacing so her Son's glory may shine forth.

CHURCH: You have shown me many faces of woman. She is mother, homemaker, friend, disciple, confidante, theologian, penitent, mystic, nurse, social activist, volunteer, missionary, evangelist, the new Eve and the enemy of Satan. I celebrate her.

WOMANSPIRIT: Yet have you fairly recognized her unique role in your own history? Without her, could you continue to grow?

CHURCH: Never! But, please, let our reflections on the past and present continue.

WOMANSPIRIT: You have given me solace and support in times of persecution, to be sure. Your documents and encyclicals uphold women's equality in dignity. You have been defender of my children, protesting against and condemning any actions that would demean my body or suppress my spirit. We have made history together, but new doors need to be opened.

CHURCH: In God's good time...

WOMANSPIRIT: But not without human effort. Your words, your teachings affect my life, my decisions, my choices, my values and goals. Could I resolve my problems without your counsel? Could my friendship with God be restored without the grace of reconciliation? Your words are imprinted on my conscience. Even when I protest, it is against your prohibitions.

CHURCH: Am I a source of conflict or peace to you?

WOMANSPIRIT: Both, of course. There are times, as in a marriage, when I can neither live with you nor without you!

CHURCH: And what makes a marriage good?

WOMANSPIRIT: You know the answer as well as I. Mutuality, partnership, dialogue, communication that aims to resolve conflicts.

CHURCH: Love, forgiveness, following a dream together, growing old side by side, living and dying together — in peace. These in the end are what make a marriage good.

WOMANSPIRIT: When you speak in this way, I know you understand what is at stake. Our friendship must never be broken. But to preach is one thing, to practice another. Look around and you will see, as I do, evidence of male domination and discrimination against women; injustice in wage-earning; the use and abuse of female bodies. Closer to home, we can visit one neighborhood church and then another and see that women are being denied participation in the ministries open to them. Poor women, immigrants and the uneducated, women of color, all worthy representatives of the church's multicultural diversity, often feel left out, on the margins of your concern. Doors are closed to study and dialogue about the question of women's ordination or the issue of birth regulation...

CHURCH: Our dialogue does not fit the category of theological discussion, though you place hard questions before me. The windows have been opened, our dear Pope John XXIII saw to that, and the Spirit blows where it will...

WOMANSPIRIT: There is no wish in me to defy your teaching authority in any way. Our tradition is my joy, too. Nothing suffices but to walk in the truth, to remain in the presence of the living God, however overwhelming our concerns may seem. This is the greatest of gifts, and legitimate authority is pledged to protect it.

CHURCH: Yet I hear a cry for more...

WOMANSPIRIT: Remain sensitive to, do not dismiss lightly, my physical, social, spiritual, psychological, intellectual, and ministerial potentials. You will see me sitting in many pews on any Sunday — more so than the men. You will notice that I am young and old, single and married, rich and indigent. I am as diverse as the continents you serve. I am in the congregation of the universal church in great numbers. Compare my attendance at ongoing formation sessions to that of the men's and you know how sincere I am about renewal.

CHURCH: You are in all of these places in great and edifying numbers. What, then, is missing?

WOMANSPIRIT: How many diocesan offices do I hold? Am I consulted on a regular basis about issues near to my heart? Do I have any voice in conclaves and curias?

CHURCH: Things are better than they were. It is a time to see doors opening. It is not a time to turn away.

WOMANSPIRIT: Where would I go? You preserve and explain the words of eternal life. You offer the word of God, the body and blood of Christ, to all humankind. You spread the Good News around the globe. Under your roof, we can share what is most precious to us: our faith.

CHURCH: You know full well the love of God has no bounds.

WOMANSPIRIT: And you know that everyone is of equal beauty in the eyes of God our Creator. Before the throne of the Most High, no one's life can be cast off like chaff in the wind. In the light of the cross of Christ, no suffering is in vain. With your best voice, you teach that all of life is good and worthy of protection from the wages of sin and death.

CHURCH: And you work at my side. You offer hope in a world scarred by war and death. You open doors to refugees and the unwanted. You feed and clothe the homeless, comfort the sick and dying.

WOMANSPIRIT: And you bless our marriages and baptize our children. You celebrate the Eucharist in open fields and in incensed cathedrals. You sing of the wonder of salvation and gather God's chosen around the altar for celebration. We must never forget this.

CHURCH: Can a mother forget her child? Can a father give sons or daughters a stone when they ask for bread? Can the God who made us ever leave us orphaned?

WOMANSPIRIT: What is your self-perception in response to these questions?

CHURCH: Sometimes I think of myself as a sleeping giant who awakens every so many years to find that the ground on which he has slept for so long without disturbance is quaking, that the world he thought he understood and protected is changing more rapidly than the speed of sound, that cohorts whom he trusted to obey him without question now want to talk over every decision. It is not easy for so big a creature to move quickly or to respond rapidly to these new insights and demands. Being so gigantic, he might trample underfoot small things that look unimportant but that may actually be upholding the entire edifice of his kingdom. The giant needs time to fully awaken and still more time to dress in fresh clothing and go abroad.

WOMANSPIRIT: That is a good story. Are you saying that in some ways our relationship is on the verge of a new beginning? That only now can the dialogue commence?

CHURCH: The breeze of change may one day blow like a mighty wind, but we must be sure our roots are intertwined at the deepest and most sure of subsoils — in the word of God and in the authority invested in us to protect Christ's teaching.

WOMANSPIRIT: Tradition is like a tree. The deeper its roots, the more it can risk to face into the wind without being swept away in a whirl of sects and schisms.

CHURCH: My heart would bleed were that day ever to come, but neither do I want the wild and beautiful winds to cease.

WOMANSPIRIT: Our faith must be full of life, not a museum piece or a bird on the way to extinction. We must find side by side with pockets of preservation peaks and valleys where the bird can leave the cage and soar free to lands of discovery where there is a plenitude of fresh food and drink.

CHURCH: There must always be places left on earth where thinking people are encouraged to press boundaries, in movements of expansion, and where guardians of truth propose boundaries to hold firm the vision through movements of contraction.

WOMANSPIRIT: Provided the quest for truth is never suppressed, we can risk to hear the Spirit's voice in these troubling times.

CHURCH: History certainly proves your point. Our sense of what is happening and God's way are not necessarily in tune. Remember when Galileo was rapidly expanding and we were stubbornly contracting?

WOMANSPIRIT: A symphony, depending on the conductor, can be as dissonant as the sound of nails scratching slate and as wondrously in tune as if the angels themselves were playing. Our history lacks equilibrium, to be sure, but that is perhaps what makes it so alive.

CHURCH: So unpredictable. And yet throughout times of peril and turmoil, amid centuries of insipid scandal, this glorious line of succession has prevailed. The center has held despite splits and cracks and divisions around the periphery.

WOMANSPIRIT: And none as devastating as that which could transpire between us.

CHURCH: There must be no chasm so wide that it cannot be crossed, no wound so deep that it cannot be healed.

WOMANSPIRIT: No exclusion so sharp-edged that a solution cannot be found. Remember our spirit lives in homes and in places of labor and leisure, inside doorways and out in fields. Look around and we are there: teaching and tidying up, preaching and praying, administering and admonishing, deciding and debating, raising questions and receiving responses, telling our story and trying to serve. We have to pull together and withstand the trauma when things fall apart. We shall not retreat to individualistic conclaves of power but respond to your call to become a community of believers.

CHURCH: Such is the Catholic way.

WOMANSPIRIT: Let us join hands lest we forget it.

Conclusion:
Enspirited Women on the Edge
of a New Era

WOMEN IN CHURCH AND SOCIETY at the end of the twentieth century continue with courage to overcome the traces of prejudice and discrimination that linger in the air like silent but deadly pollution. There are laws in place that assure women equal treatment in the workplace and mutual respect in the home. Violence against women, sexual harassment, pornographic exploitation — all such evils are sinful and liable to prosecution. By contrast, women's real contributions in the home and to society are exemplary and worthy of the highest praise.

Yet for all this progress, there is still much to be done by and for women if Gospel values are to be at the center of life and world. Women writers and scholars, teachers and speakers, both in America and around the globe, dare to press the boundaries of thought. Philosophers explore the meaning of equality in dignity. Christian anthropologists question false assumptions that hamper our understanding of what it means to be males and females made in the image and likeness of God. Sociologists examine oppressive structures that block human rights and despoil the ideal of justice and liberty for all. Psychologists probe the attitudes and actions that support discriminatory structures and call for deep conversion of heart. Theologians propose necessary changes in the light of the revelation. Spiritual guides work to restore faith in womanspirit as a distinct manifestation of God's own spirit, alive from age to age in the human race.

If we are on the edge of a new era of faith — and I firmly believe this to be the case — then enspirited women are leading the way. Over the past twenty-five years, women have been described as alienated, marginalized, fragmented, and victimized. Now is the time to let go of these labels. Women resist either/or categories. We combine emotion and reason, imagination and intelligence, contemplation and action. Most of us resist identification with one or the other extreme group. None of us wants to be split like taut zippers between the forces of conservatism and liberalism, traditionalism and futurism. We do not relish living life as if it were a tug of war between bellicose tribes. Some camps despise women for being shy and demure, others for being bold and assertive. One group wants us to be polite and pleasing; the other tells us to push toward power and promotion. I, for one, am tired of it. This useless war of words wearies womanspirit. Labels are not impressive. I feel ashamed when issue-bound women are incapable of being civil to one another, when our own kind fights for turf and argues to the death about each one's own version of women's rights, when to win a point means hurting and hating one's sisters.

What a waste of time and energy these skirmishes are. It is as if we have allowed a martial mentality, depleted of faith, hope, and love, to herd us into camps for the fearful, the despondent, the driven, the dependent, the dominant, the indulgent, the sentimental, the serious. None of these "dogtags" are worthy descriptions of enspirited women. Each points to perhaps an aspect of our personality; none can possibly capture the whole.

What is this illusive yet real spirit of which I speak? Even at the end of this book, I am only beginning to understand it myself. I have followed a few clues. I have made some guesses. I have uncovered a hint or two in my readings and meetings, but the spirit of Christian womanhood is still unfolding. Perhaps another memory will illustrate what I am trying to say.

It is early morning. The mist rises like incense from the ripples on the lake. Our hooks are baited, our lines cast. We whisper "Good luck" to each other and wait. It is one of those magical mornings children never forget. The first bass is reeled in by my father, then I catch one, my brothers each get two, and we are elated. It is my turn to put them on the stringer, and there they flop in a small school by the shoreline. Then the excitement is over. We try new lures and bait but nothing happens. By sunrise we have walked downstream, away from our initial catch. In the meantime Mother has been by our campsite preparing coffee. She walks to the shore, looks into the water, and her heart leaps. She will show us! Here we are trying to catch fish and a whole school has come to her. She sneaks back to the station wagon to find the fishing net. It's not there! She is undaunted. Sleek as a jaguar stalking its prey, she slinks to the shore. She will scoop them up in her bare hands — becoming the first person in our family to perform such a feat. She waits for the right moment, holds her breath and in triumph swoops up the whole school. She shouts her victory call to the rest of us. We run toward her just as she sees the stringer. Her mouth drops in shock as the five of us crack up over the twice-caught fish, laughing until our stomachs ache. What was wonderful is that Mother could laugh at herself. She told the story to many relatives and friends, enjoying with each embellishment the humor in it.

I hope women never lose their love of laughter. A sense of play is so important. Without a capacity to let go and laugh at ourselves, we lose our perspective. What shrivels first is our sense of adventure, our conviction that we can catch fish with no bait, that we can chain chaos by the ecstasy of creative ideas.

Without laughter our lives become too tense. And for what reason? All the seriousness in the world, a multitude of fingers worked to the bone, will not make a difference or keep us sane or initiate effective change unless we live to enjoy what we have accomplished.

I make myself look in the mirror in the morning before I put on the face I need to face the world. I smile purposefully lest lines of worry and frowns of fear make me forget how funny life really is. I need to release unnecessary signs of stress, and no remedy is as good as laughter. Humor puts problems in perspective. Even elephants can slip on banana peels. Who is in charge of the world after all? God must laugh heartily when I pretend to an importance that is as ludicrous as catching caught fish.

Humor is redemptive. It restores humility. It reminds us that we are really only *humus*, here today and definitely gone tomorrow! I am not trying to mitigate the magnitude of what women in our era are trying to accomplish. I want only to reduce the facial wrinkles caused by stress and tension that obscure the restoring power of redemptive humor. We women need to worry less and laugh more, lest we lose touch with the energizing power of the spirit.

Touch, like play, is another point of contact with the creativity of God. As Mary held and caressed Jesus, so must women embrace the Christ in others who need their love. We live in a world that believes in keeping people at a safe distance. I am sensitive to how stiff bodies can be, because I grew up in a formative tradition that believes in bodily contact, hearty hugs, love pats, and back tickles.

Genuine touch, chaste yet loving, compassionate yet purposeful, cannot be forced. The power that resides in such exchanges cannot help but signify the difference between enspirited and dispirited women and men. When a Mother Teresa of Calcutta cradles a dying person in her arms, gratitude makes even a skeletal face glow. I worked with a woman once who, after visiting my family, confessed in tears that she grew up with parents who touched her as little as possible. She admitted passing from one lover to another from the time she was a teenager, pathetically trying to satisfy an abyss of need no one could fill.

Women not only need to laugh heartily — in the spirit of a Julian of Norwich — they need to become more chaste and faithful married and single lovers. We cannot move into a new era of appreciation and respect for each person's dignity and gifts unless we choose to love as Jesus did.

Love is our strongest weapon against the forces of oppression and hate. We must continue to believe this because the only alternative is to become what we most oppose: disrespectful, controlling people, who press labels on those with whom they do not agree, who withdraw their love at the first sign of trouble or use its power to seduce and manipulate the weak.

To touch chastely another heart is to set a person free; it is to will her or him to be. This kind of enspirited turning to another in need is a gift that will be returned to us a hundredfold. It will melt away the armor of fear with which we encase our heart. It will release the unique truth of who we are — a truth that needs to be cultivated if the child within us is to stay alive.

As the Word became flesh and dwelt among us in a gesture of pure love, so must we enflesh the Christ in us in hands that heal, in eyes that confirm, in words that redeem.

If laughter and love characterize enspirited, enfleshed women, then so too do words that vow to remain honest, whatever the cost, be it lost popularity or outright pain. Women's words must give witness to God's promise of justice, peace, and mercy for all people. What we choose to say, what we hold in silence, will have significant repercussions in this time of reassessment of values, dreams, and directions.

Words are not casual flares like fireworks on the Fourth of July. They have power: to heal and hurt, free and ensnare, create and destroy, affirm and attack. Women need not be afraid to share their feelings, condemn falsehood, and call for honesty in all social circles.

Speaking can become like water running wild after a fierce storm if it is not tempered in silence. The right rhythm of words spoken and words withheld is a sign that women and men are in tune with the transcendent force of their spirit, not merely with their functional bent to plan and project. Words tended like a garden will bear good fruit. Words harvested too quickly, with no time for quiet assessment, may produce only a withered crop, lacking the nutrients to feed a population starving for solid food.

Women must be careful not to become victims of deceptive propaganda they rightfully despise. Language is as central an issue as laughter and love in this enspirited era we are entering. Words can only catch fire if the fuel we use is ready to burn. We have to choose our words wisely. We have to be sure they are rooted in the firm soil of our faith tradition. We need to examine with candor and courage what in us has become deformed by the smooth, seductive rhetoric of false spiritualities and ideologies that erode a gospel vision.

On the edge of a new era, one in which testaments of faith may be more important than quests for power, we must be willing to wait upon God's word before we act, just as women wait for a child to be born. The time is approaching for needed change to occur. We must not rush the butterfly of transformation or it will emerge with shriveled wings. Before creativity reorders chaos, there is a period when things seem to be hopeless and out of control, a time when nothing seems to be stirring like mist on a morning lake. It is easy to grow discouraged when, despite the best bait and tackle, the fish do not bite. This is the between time that always precedes a new era.

It is as if earth itself is in an incubator, as if the whole of life is on probation, groaning for release. We want to cling to old ways, but they are gone forever. We envision new avenues of freedom, but we have as yet not been able to lay the foundations on which these highways can stretch to the far horizon. We want to let go of our security blankets, but there are few, if any, replacements in sight. It is the between time.

We feel as if we are stepping over a cliff's edge about to plunge into the unknown, so we step back just when everything in us wants to leap over the precipice and enjoy the view that awaits us on the other side. It is the between time.

We are like children setting off for a walk in the woods, leaving our fears aside for the moment and actually relishing the sense of danger. We do not know what unknowns we will have to face or if we will receive more than we bargained for. That is a risk we have to take if we want to remain enspirited women who seek the wild blue yonder.

The current form of our life may be in as much disarray as a beach after a hurricane, but enspirited women have never minded the challenge of making something out of nothing. There could be no edge and certainly no new era without a time of loss, suffering, confusion, polarization, and disorientation.

In the between time we feel baffled by people who keep putting the barnacles back on the ship when we want to see it catch sail outside the harbor. We want to fly with the wind on the open sea. The powers that be want to drop anchor. It is the time between preparation and action. It can be terribly frustrating for enspirited women to wait for yet another season to make the journey to freedom.

Once, without the guidance of my friend, who had lived for years in the Arizona desert, I set out alone for what was to be an early morning walk. I followed trails in the sand cut by cattle and found myself climbing up what looked like a small knoll but soon became a high hill. I reached up for a hand hold and saw to my disbelief that I had come within inches of touching a nesting snake, whose species I had no interest in ascertaining. I tumbled backward for a short distance before regaining my balance and ran in the other direction. That was when I realized I had lost sight of the ranch and really did not know where I was. I felt my heart beat faster because I had no wilderness training to speak of, only some ancient Girl Scout lore about staying calm and checking the angle of the sun. It was fully risen by this time so I knew east from west, but was that enough to bring me home? I took a deep breath, found an open space to sit, away from rocks and dense vegetation, and ate the orange I had luckily thought to put in my jacket pocket as I left the house. I knew from whence I had come. I was not sure where I was going. I felt disoriented, like a person half awake and half asleep, like a blindfolded pilgrim being led by the spirit to a place of revelation.

I wanted to leave the wilderness and return to the comforts of the ranch, but I also wanted to go deeper into the desert, to feel really empty, hungry, dependent on my wits and divine wisdom, on the edge of life and death. It was an odd sensation since all I was doing was sucking the last bits of juice from my orange. Still I knew on a deeper level of reality that there are no superficial answers to the mystery of survival in a universe greater than we are. The desert does not allow people to play games. I had to be careful. I had to watch where I was walking, reconstruct my steps without losing the inner freedom I felt.

I started hiking west toward what I thought was the road home, searching for my earlier footsteps like an Indian scout. There was a moment when a tempting trail veered to the right. I wanted to take it. The wildness of a journey into the darkness of not knowing appealed to my bohemian side, but good sense prevailed, and I stuck to the, by now, familiar trail.

My friend was about to set out after me when I happily rapped on the kitchen door, eager to share the adventure. I was prepared to receive a gentle scolding since I had gone out without wearing the proper hat or walking boots, yet she could not help but agree that I had had a chance to test out what could happen when I trusted God and allowed grace to erase futile fears.

I learned from this experience that enspirited women will always see affliction as a gift advancing our capacity for appreciative abandonment to the mystery. We want to make sense out of what appears to make no sense at all. Enspirited women know that there is no way out of the wilderness of ignorance and depletion but the way through to a new era of spiritual reformation and repletion.

Women of spirit must learn to trust direct, experiential knowledge while submitting what we discover to the test of reality. Along the way we need to remain, as Jesus says, wise as serpents and gentle as doves. We have to trust that there is always a freshness in God's call, that no pain is without transforming potential. Grace urges us to complete what we have begun. It prompts us to prayer and effective action. Change will not last unless it flows from contemplation.

I worry when we women complain that we are too busy to pray, that we have no time to do spiritual reading, that we cannot spare a few moments, even while waiting in line, to meditate. We must operate from a serene center to put into motion a society less prejudiced, a church more alert to women's gifts for ministry, banishing all forms of discrimination, and initiating a phase of collaborative leadership that will characterize the next two thousand years of Christianity.

I know we are ready to move away from worn-out structures without losing our foundations. A new era of faith, hope, and love is around the corner. As when wild geese hear the call to migrate to a warmer climate, so women hear God calling and feel our hearts stir within.

Womanspirit wanders through the world, seeking a place where people stop hurting one another for no reason, a dream world where the wolf and the lamb live in peace together. We envision what God saw when the Son came among us, born of woman, willing to suffer for the sake of truth yet destined to rise to glory.

May we unite our spirit to the spirit of Jesus, to the courageous heart of Mary. May we move church and society by leaps and bounds into the land of likeness to the divine forming mystery from whence all creation came. May the blessing of God almighty be upon us. May we advance unafraid into an era that belongs in a special way to womanspirit. May we reclaim the deep feminine in our human spirituality.

Bibliography

Anthony, Edd, and Curtis W. Johnson. *Faith and Fame*. Huntington, Ind.: Our Sunday Visitor, 1989.

Armstrong, Christopher. *Evelyn Underhill*. Grand Rapids, Mich.: William B. Eerdmans Publishing Co., 1975.

Ascher, Barbara L. *The Habit of Loving*. New York: Random House, 1989.

Atkinson, Clarissa W., Constance W. Buchanan, and Margaret R. Miles. *Immaculate and Powerful: The Female in Sacred Image and Social Reality*. Boston: Beacon Press, 1985.

Baldwin, Anne B. *Catherine of Siena*. Huntington, Ind.: Our Sunday Visitor, 1987.

Brokenness: The Stories of Six Women Whose Faith Grew in Crisis. Cincinnati: St. Anthony Messenger Press, 1980.

Borriello, Luigi, O.C.D. *Spiritual Doctrine of Blessed Elizabeth of the Trinity*. New York: Alba House, 1986.

Brownmiller, Susan. *Femininity*. New York: Fawcett Columbine, 1984.

Brown, Raymond E., Karl P. Donfried, Joseph A. Fitzmyer, and John Reumann. *Mary in the New Testament*. Philadelphia: Fortress, 1978.

Buby, Bertrand, S.M. *Mary the Faithful Disciple*. New York: Paulist Press, 1985.

Byrne, Lavinia. *Women before God: Our Own Spirituality*. Mystic, Conn.: Twenty-Third Publications, 1988.

Buytendijk, F. J. J. *Woman: A Contemporary View*. Glen Rock, N.J.: Newman Press, 1968.

Carr, Anne E. *Transforming Grace: Christian Tradition and Women's Experience*. San Francisco: Harper & Row, 1988.

Catherine of Genoa. *Purgation and Purgatory, the Spiritual Dialogue*. Trans. Serge Hughes. Classics of Western Spirituality. New York: Paulist Press, 1979.

Catherine of Siena. *The Dialogue*. Trans. Suzanne Noffke. Classics of Western Spirituality. New York: Paulist Press, 1980.

Celeste, Marie, Sr. *The Intimate Friendships of Elizabeth Ann Bayley Seton*. New York: Alba House, 1989.

Chervin, Ronda, and Mary Neill. *Bringing the Mother with You*. New York: Seabury Press, 1982.

———. *The Woman's Tale: A Journal of Inner Exploration*. New York: Crossroad, 1980.

Chittister, Joan, O.S.B. *Imaging God/Women's Experience.* Silver Springs, Md.: Leadership Conference of Women Religious, 1988.

Christ, Carol P. *Diving Deep and Surfacing: Women Writers on Spiritual Quest.* Boston: Beacon Press, 1980.

Clissold, Stephen. *St. Teresa of Avila.* London: Sheldon Press, 1979.

Condon, Jane. *A Half Step Behind.* New York: Dodd, Mead, 1985.

Cooper, Patricia, and Norma Bradley Allen. *The Quilters: Women and Domestic Art, An Oral History.* New York: Doubleday, 1989.

Day, Dorothy. *Therese.* Springfield, Ill.: Templegate Publishers, 1979.

Daily Readings with Julian of Norwich. Vol. 1. Springfield, Ill.: Templegate, 1980.

Daily Readings with Julian of Norwich. Vol. 2. Ed. Robert Llewelyn. Springfield, Ill.: Templegate, 1986.

Deen, Edith. *All of the Women of the Bible.* San Francisco: Harper & Row, 1983.

Dickinson, Emily. *The Poetry of Emily Dickinson.* Middletown, Conn.: Wesleyan University Press, 1968.

Dillard, Annie. *Pilgrim at Tinker Creek.* New York: Bantam Books, 1974.

―――. *Teaching a Stone to Talk.* New York: Harper & Row, 1982.

Doherty, Catherine de Hueck. *Our Lady's Unknown Mysteries.* Denville, N.J.: Dimension Books, 1979.

Doyle, Brendan. *Meditations with Julian of Norwich.* Santa Fe, N.M.: Bear, 1983.

Durvin, Joseph I. *Mrs. Seton: Foundress of the American Sisters of Charity.* New York: Farrar, Straus & Giroux, 1975.

Elizabeth of the Trinity. *The Complete Works.* Vol. 1. Trans. Sr. Aletheia Kane, O.C.D. Washington, D.C.: Institute of Carmelite Studies, 1984.

Fatula, Mary Ann. *Catherine of Siena's Way.* Wilmington, Del.: Michael Glazier, 1987.

Fiedler, Leslie. *Simone Weil: Waiting for God.* New York: Harper & Row, 1951.

Fiorenza, Elizabeth Schüssler. *In Memory of Her.* New York: Crossroad, 1985.

Fitzgerald, Sally, ed. *Letters of Flannery O'Connor: The Habit of Being.* New York: Farrar, Straus & Giroux, 1979.

Foley, Nadine, O.P. *Claiming Our Truth: Reflections on Identity by United States Women Religious.* Washington, D.C.: Leadership Conference of Women Religious, 1988.

Fox, Matthew. *Illuminations of Hildegard of Bingen.* Santa Fe, N.M.: Bear, 1985.

Francis and Clare. *The Complete Works.* Trans. Regis J. Armstrong, O.F.M., and Ignatius C. Brady, O.F.M. New York: Paulist Press, 1982.

Frank, Anne. *The Diary of a Young Girl.* Trans. B. M. Mooyaart-Doubleday. New York: Modern Library, 1952.

Furlong, Monica. *Therese of Lisieux.* New York: Pantheon Books, 1987.

Gaucher, Guy. *The Story of a Life: Saint Thérèse of Lisieux.* San Francisco: Harper & Row, 1982.

Garvin, Paul. *The Life and Sayings of Saint Catherine of Genoa.* New York: Alba House, 1964.

Giordani, Igino. *Saint Catherine of Siena.* Boston: Daughters of St. Paul, 1975.

Goricheva, Tatiana. *Talking about God Is Dangerous.* New York: Crossroad, 1988.

Greene, Dana. *Evelyn Underhill: Artist of the Infinite Life.* New York: Crossroad, 1990.

Guyon, Madame. *Experiencing the Depths of Jesus Christ.* Augusta, Me.: Christian Books, 1981.

Hadewijch. *The Complete Works.* Trans. Mother Columba Hart, O.S.B. New York: Paulist Press, 1980.

Haskell, Molly. *Love and Other Infectious Diseases: A Memoir.* New York: Wm. Morrow, 1990.

Haughton, Rosemary. *The Catholic Thing.* Springfield, Ill.: Templegate, 1980.

————. *The Passionate God.* New York: Paulist Press, 1981.

Hellman, John. *Simone Weil: An Introduction to Her Thought.* Philadelphia: Fortress Press, 1982.

Herbstrith, Waltraud. *Edith Stein: A Biography.* San Francisco: Harper & Row, 1971.

Hillesum, Etty. *An Interrupted Life: The Diaries of Etty Hillesum, 1941–1943.* Trans. Arnold J. Pomerans. New York: Pantheon Books, 1983.

————. *Letters from Westerbork.* Trans. Arnold J. Pomerans. New York: Pantheon Books, 1986.

Houselander, Caryll. *The Reed of God.* New York: Sheed & Ward, 1944.

I, Catherine. Trans. Kenelm Foster, O.P., and Mary John Ronayne, O.P. St. James, London: Collins, 1980.

Janda, J. *Julian.* New York: Seabury Press, 1984.

Jamart, François, O.C.D. *Complete Spiritual Doctrine of St. Thérèse of Lisieux.* New York: Alba House, 1961.

Julian of Norwich. *Showings.* Trans. Edmund Colledge, O.S.A., and James Walsh, S.J. New York: Paulist Press, 1978.

Keyes, Frances Parkinson. *St. Thérèse of Lisieux.* London: Eyre & Spottiswoode, 1951.

Kolbenschlag, Madonna. *Kiss Sleeping Beauty Good-Bye: Breaking the Spell of Feminine Myths and Models.* Garden City, N.Y.: Doubleday & Co., 1979.

————. *Women in the Church I*. Washington, D.C.: Pastoral Press, 1987.

L'Engle, Madeleine. *A Circle of Quiet*. Book 1. *The Crosswicks Journal*. San Francisco: Harper & Row, 1972.

————. *The Summer of the Great-Grandmother*. Book 2. *The Crosswicks Journal*. San Francisco: Harper & Row, 1974.

————. *The Irrational Season*. Book 3. *The Crosswicks Journal*. San Francisco: Harper & Row, 1977.

————. *Two-Part Invention: The Story of a Marriage*. San Francisco: Harper & Row, 1988.

Letters of St. Louise de Marillac. Trans. Sister Helen Marie Law. Emmitsburg, Md.: St. Joseph's Provincial House Press, 1972.

Lincoln, Victoria. *Teresa: A Woman*. Albany: State University of New York Press, 1984.

Lindbergh, Anne Morrow. *Gift from the Sea*. New York: Vintage Books, Random House, 1965.

Llewelyn, Robert. *All Shall Be Well*. New York: Paulist Press, 1982.

Martin, Faith. *Call Me Blessed*. Grand Rapids, Mich.: William B. Eerdmans, 1988.

Milhaven, Annie Lally. *The Inside Stories*. Mystic, Conn.: Twenty-Third, 1987.

Molinari, Paul, S.J. *Julian of Norwich: The Teaching of a 14th Century Mystic*. London: Longmans, Green and Co., 1958.

Morrison, Toni. *Song of Solomon*. New York: Alfred A. Knopf, 1978.

Muggeridge, Malcolm. *Something Beautiful for God*. London: Collins/ Fontana Books, 1974.

Muto, Susan. *A Practical Guide to Spiritual Reading*. Denville, N.J.: Dimension Books, 1976.

————. *Blessings That Make Us Be: Living the Beatitudes*. New York: Crossroad, 1982. Rpt. Petersham, Mass.: St. Bede's, 1991.

————. *Celebrating the Single Life: A Spirituality for Single Persons in Today's World*. New York: Doubleday, 1982. Rpt. New York: Crossroad, 1989.

————. *Meditation in Motion*. New York: Doubleday, 1986.

————. *John of the Cross for Today: The Ascent*. Notre Dame, Ind.: Ave Maria Press, 1990.

Muto, Susan, and Adrian van Kaam. *Commitment: Key to Christian Maturity*. Mahwah, N.J.: Paulist Press, 1989.

Myers, Rawley. *American Women of Faith*. Huntington, Ind.: Our Sunday Visitor, 1989.

Noffke, Suzanne, O.P. *The Prayers of Catherine of Siena*. New York: Paulist Press, 1983.

Nunnally-Cox, Janice. *Fore-Mothers: Women of the Bible*. New York: Seabury Press, 1981.

Oben, Freda Mary. *Edith Stein: Scholar, Feminist, Saint*. New York: Alba House, 1988.

O'Brien, Theresa King. *The Spiral Path: Essays and Interviews on Women's Spirituality*. St. Paul, Minn.: YES International, 1988.

Ochs, Carol. *Women and Spirituality*. Totowa, N.J.: Rowman & Allanheld, 1983.

O'Connor, Flannery. *Everything That Rises Must Converge*. New York: Noonday, div. of Farrar, Straus & Giroux, 1961.

O'Connor, Patricia. *In Search of Therese*. Wilmington, Del.: Michael Glazier, 1987.

Petrement, Simone. *Simone Weil*. New York: Random House, 1988.

Philipon, M. M., O.P. *Sister Elizabeth of the Trinity*. Westminster, Md.: Newman Press, 1955.

Plaskow, Judith, and Carol P. Christ. *Womanspirit Rising: A Feminist Reader in Religion*. San Francisco: Harper & Row, 1979.

———. *Weaving the Vision: New Patterns in Feminist Spirituality*. San Francisco: Harper & Row, 1989.

Powers, Jessica. *Selected Poetry of Jessica Powers*. Ed. Regina Siegfried and Robert Morneau. Kansas City, Mo.: Sheed & Ward, 1989.

Puls, Joan, O.S.F. *Every Bush Is Burning: A Spirituality for Our Times*. Mystic, Conn.: Twenty-Third, 1985.

Raymond of Capua. *The Life of Catherine of Siena*. Wilmington, Del.: Michael Glazier, 1980.

Rix, Sara E. *The American Woman, 1987–88*. New York: W. W. Norton, 1987.

———. *The American Woman, 1988–89*. New York: W. W. Norton, 1988.

Rosewell, Pamela. *The Five Silent Years of Corrie Ten Boom*. Grand Rapids, Mich.: Zondervan, 1986.

Rubin, Lillian B. *Intimate Strangers: Men and Women Together*. New York: Harper & Row, 1983.

Ruether, Rosemary Radford. *Womanguides: Readings toward a Feminist Theology*. Boston: Beacon Press, 1985.

Seton, Elizabeth. *Selected Writings*. Ed. Ellin Kelly and Annabelle Melville. In *Sources of American Spirituality*. Mahwah, N.J.: Paulist Press, 1987.

Schneiders, Sandra M. *Women and the Word*. New York: Paulist Press, 1986.

Shank, Lillian Thoma, and John A. Nichols. *Peaceweavers: Medieval Religious Women*. Washington, D.C.: Cistercian, 1987.

Sharma, Arvind. *Women in World Religions*. New York: State University of New York, 1987.

Sister Gesualda of the Holy Spirit. *St. Theresa, The Little Flower*. Boston: St. Paul Editions, 1973.

Stein, Edith. *Life in a Jewish Family, 1891–1916*. Vol. 1. *The Collected Works of Edith Stein*. Trans. Josephine Koppel, O.C.D. Washington, D.C.: ICS, 1986.

――――. *Woman: Collected Works of Edith Stein*. Vol. 2. Trans. Freda Mary Oben. Washington, D.C.: Institute of Carmelite Studies, 1987.

Stratton, Joanna L. *Pioneer Women: Voices from the Kansas Frontier*. New York: Simon & Schuster, 1981.

Ten Boom, Corrie. *The Hiding Place*. Great Britain: Hodder and Stoughton, 1972.

――――. *Tramp for the Lord*. New York: Pillar Books, 1976.

Teresa of Avila. *Collected Works*. Vol. 1. Trans. Kieran Kavanaugh, O.C.D., and Otilio Rodriguez, O.C.D. Washington, D.C.: Institute of Carmelite Studies, 1976.

――――. *The Interior Castle*. Trans. Kieran Kavanaugh and Otilio Rodriguez. Classics of Western Spirituality. New York: Paulist Press, 1979.

――――. *Collected Works*. Vol. 2. Trans. Kieran Kavanaugh, O.C.D., and Otilio Rodriguez, O.C.D. Washington, D.C.: Institute of Carmelite Studies, 1985.

――――. *Collected Works*. Vol. 3. Trans. Kieran Kavanaugh, O.C.D., and Otilio Rodriguez, O.C.D. Washington, D.C.: Institute of Carmelite Studies, 1985.

Thérèse of Lisieux. *Collected Letters*. Trans. F. J. Sheed. London: Sheed & Ward, 1972.

――――. *Story of a Soul*. Trans. John Clarke, O.C.D. Washington, D.C.: Institute of Carmelite Studies, 1975.

――――. *Her Last Conversations*. Trans. John Clarke, O.C.D. Washington, D.C.: Institute of Carmelite Studies, 1977.

――――. *General Correspondence*. Trans. John Clarke, O.C.D. Washington, D.C.: Institute of Carmelite Studies, 1982.

Thoreau, Henry David. *Walden and Civil Disobedience*. Ed. Sherman Paul. Boston: Houghton Mifflin, 1960.

Thoughts of Edith Stein. Trans. Carmel of Maria Regina. Eugene, Ore.: Four Corners Press, 1986.

Timmerman, Joan. *The Mardi Gras Syndrome: Rethinking Christian Sexuality*. New York: Crossroad, 1985.

Uhlein, Gabriele. *Meditations with Hildegard of Bingen*. Santa Fe, N.M.: Bear, 1983.

Underhill, Evelyn. *Practical Mysticism*. New York: E. P. Dutton, 1943.

――――. *Mysticism: A Study in the Nature and Development of Man's Spiritual Consciousness*. New York: E. P. Dutton, 1961.

van Kaam, Adrian, C.S.Sp. *Spirituality and the Gentle Life*. Denville, N.J.: Dimension Books, 1975.

――――. *The Woman at the Well*. Denville, N.J.: Dimension Books, 1976.

――――. *The Science of Formative Spirituality: Fundamental Formation*. Vol. 1. New York: Crossroad, 1983.

――――. *Roots of Christian Joy*. Denville, N.J.: Dimension Books, 1985.

———. *The Science of Formative Spirituality: Fundamental Formation.* Vol. 2. New York: Crossroad, 1985.

———. *The Science of Formative Spirituality: Formation of the Human Heart.* Vol. 3. New York: Crossroad, 1986.

———. *The Science of Formative Spirituality: Scientific Formation.* Vol. 4. New York: Crossroad, 1987.

Vinck, Jose De. *Revelations of Women Mystics.* New York: Alba House, 1985.

Walker, Alice. *The Color Purple.* New York: Washington Square Press, 1982.

Weaver, Mary Jo. *New Catholic Women: A Contemporary Challenge to Traditional Religious Authority.* San Francisco: Harper & Row, 1985.

Weil, Simone. *Waiting for God.* New York: Harper & Row, 1951.

———. *Gateway to God.* Great Britain: Fontana Books, 1974.

White, George Abbott. *Simone Weil: Interpretations of a Life.* Amherst: University of Massachusetts Press, 1981.

Wolski, Joann Conn. *Women's Spirituality: Resources for Christian Development.* New York: Paulist Press, 1986.

Woodruff, Sue. *Meditations with Mechtild of Magdeburg.* Santa Fe, N.M.: Bear, 1982.

Wright, Wendy M. *Bond of Perfection: Jeanne de Chantal and François de Sales.* New York: Paulist Press, 1985.